Twayne's United States Authors Series

Sylvia E. Bowman, *Editor*

INDIANA UNIVERSITY

Charles Brockden Brown

CHARLES BROCKDEN BROWN

By DONALD A. RINGE

University of Kentucky

 **98**

Twayne Publishers, Inc.   ::   New York

For
DONNY AND JIMMY

Preface

THIS BOOK OFFERS the reader a detailed analysis and critical evaluation of the novels of Charles Brockden Brown. Though it recognizes the historical importance of his books as the first truly significant novels written in America and points out some of the ways in which they foreshadow later American fiction, its focus is not historical. Neither is it much concerned with the sources of Brown's ideas. Background information and biographical data are, of course, used where pertinent; but the controlling purpose is fundamentally critical: to understand and evaluate the books so that we may arrive at a just estimate of Brown's success as a writer of fiction.

Although the arrangement is chronological, the book is by no means a biography of Brown. Five of the seven chapters cover only a very brief period of his life, 1798 to 1801, the years of his intense artistic creation. What went before and after is merely summarized in the opening and closing chapters. Such an allocation of space is justified by the fact that only Brown's major fiction has a claim to our critical attention today. Detailed discussion of his experience as editor, annalist, and political pamphleteer, therefore, was considered to be beyond the scope of this study. Hence, this material is given only the briefest treatment in the pages that follow.

For details of Brown's life, I have relied in general upon the published biographies, most particularly that by Harry R. Warfel, the best and most reliable of the three. Where scholars disagree on important facts of Brown's life, I have noted the major differences in the footnotes. A small amount of good critical work on Brown has begun to appear during the last few years. My debt to recent critics who have published significant studies is apparent both in the text and in the footnotes.

In writing this book, I have, of course, incurred a number of personal debts that I am happy to acknowledge. I am especially grateful to Professor Harry R. Warfel, who not only answered my questions on details of Brown's career, but also generously provided me with copies of the footnotes to his biography of

Brown, which was published with only a general note on the sources. Librarians at both the University Library and the William L. Clements Library at the University of Michigan were always helpful, and the following institutions have made Brown materials available to me: Tufts University Library, Oberlin College Library, The New York Public Library, and the Midwest Inter-library Center. Sylvia E. Bowman, of course, edited the manuscript; and a patient wife lent her assistance in ways that only she can fully understand.

D. A. R.

Ann Arbor, Michigan
January, 1964

Contents

Chronology

1771   Charles Brockden Brown born January 17 in Philadelphia.

1781-   Attended Friends' Latin School in Philadelphia until 1786
1786   or 1787.

1787-   Studied law in the office of Alexander Wilcocks, but
1792   abandoned the profession in 1792 (or perhaps 1793) before he had practiced it. Was a member of the Belles
Lettres Club. Published "The Rhapsodist," a series of
four essays, in the Philadelphia *Columbian Magazine* in
1789. Met Elihu Hubbard Smith, who had come to Philadelphia in 1790-1791 to study medicine.

1793-   During the Philadelphia yellow fever epidemic of 1793,
1796   visited Smith in Connecticut. In 1794, visited in New
York, where Smith was practicing medicine. Became acquainted with the members of the Friendly Club, especially William Dunlap, whom he visited in Perth Amboy
in 1795 and 1796. Wrote a poem called "Devotion" in
1794. Began a "Philadelphia novel"—possibly the beginning of *Arthur Mervyn*—in 1795. Moved to New York in
the late summer of 1796.

1797   Returned to Philadelphia in March. Completed *Sky-Walk*
by the end of the year, but this novel was never published.

1798   Published a number of short pieces, including the beginning of *Arthur Mervyn* in the Philadelphia *Weekly Magazine*. Published *Alcuin*, Parts I and II, in April. Arrived in
New York for an extended visit in July. Published *Wieland* in September. Withdrew to Perth Amboy after
Smith's death of the yellow fever and his own illness
with the disease. Left for Philadelphia in October and
returned to New York in November.

1799   Published *Ormond* early in the year; the first part of
Arthur Mervyn by spring; *Edgar Huntly* in the summer.
In April, began to publish *The Monthly Magazine and
American Review*.

1800   Published the second part of *Arthur Mervyn* in the summer; the last issue of *The Monthly Magazine* in December. Returned to Philadelphia late in the year and became associated with his brothers' mercantile business.

1801   Published *Clara Howard* in the summer; *Jane Talbot* later in the year. Toured the Hudson to Albany and returned through Massachusetts and Connecticut.

1803   Engaged in political pamphleteering: published *An Address to the Government of the United States on the Cession of Louisiana to the French* in January; *Monroe's Embassy; or, The Conduct of the Government in Relation to Our Claims to the Navigation of the Mississippi* in March. In September, began to publish *The Literary Magazine and American Register*, which he continued to edit at least through 1806.

1804   Married Elizabeth Linn, November 19. To them were born three sons and one daughter. Published a translation of Volney's *A View of the Soil and Climate of the United States*.

1805   Published "Sketch of the Life and Character of John Blair Linn," his wife's brother, as an introduction to Linn's poem, *Valerian*.

1806   The mercantile firm dissolved.

1807   Published a political pamphlet, *The British Treaty of Commerce and Navigation*. Began to publish *The American Register, or General Repository of History, Politics, and Science*, of which five semi-annual volumes appeared between 1807 and his death.

1809   Published a political pamphlet, *An Address to the Congress of the United States on the Utility and Justice of Restrictions upon Foreign Commerce* in January.

1810   Died, most probably on February 21, in Philadelphia.

Charles Brockden Brown

CHAPTER 1

Prelude

IN A TRULY ASTONISHING BURST of creative activity, Charles Brockden Brown published in less than a year the four novels for which he is best remembered. Writing at what must have been a high degree of intensity, Brown completed *Wieland, Ormond,* the first part of *Arthur Mervyn,* and *Edgar Huntly* between the summer of 1798 and that of 1799; and, within the next two years or so, he ended his brief career as a novelist with the second part of *Arthur Mervyn,* and with *Clara Howard,* and *Jane Talbot.* Any consideration of Brown as a literary artist must, therefore, concentrate on the remarkable period from 1798 to 1801 when his major work appeared. Everything before was prelude; what remained was largely anticlimax. To be sure, Brown had been writing for many years before the publication of *Wieland* in 1798. His first published work, a poem and a series of four undistinguished essays, had appeared as early as 1789;[1] and he continued to write—magazine material, political pamphlets, and volumes of annals—almost to the time of his death at the age of thirty-nine in 1810. But, from the point of view of American literary history, only the half dozen novels have any real importance. Only they command the attention of the serious student of American literature.

I *Critical Estimates*

There can be no question that Brown's work is historically significant, for it marks the starting point of American fiction. Nothing like *Wieland* or *Edgar Huntly* had yet appeared in America, and it was almost a generation before any American novelist would again write so much and so well. Brown stands virtually alone at the beginning of the nineteenth century, for only Hugh Henry Brackenridge among contemporary American

novelists enjoys much critical esteem; and Brown's importance
is surely the greater because he foreshadows so much of what
was to come. Critics have seen in his work adumbrations of many
other American writers; and Cooper, Hawthorne, and Poe are
most frequently said to have been in his debt. Indeed, recent
scholars have gone even further. Richard Chase has seen in
"Brown's elevated rhetoric and his melodramatic effects" a fore-
cast of "much that is admirable" in later American writers of
fiction, including "Melville, Faulkner, and even James."[2] And
R. W. B. Lewis finds in the character of Arthur Mervyn the first
appearance of a "representative hero" who was to recur in the
works of many subsequent American authors.[3] Clearly, Brown's
novels demand attention if only because of their importance in
the development of American literary art.

Historical significance, however, is not their only claim to our
attention; for many readers have attested to their literary value.
Writers as diverse as Keats, Shelley, Poe, Prescott, Hawthorne,
Whittier, and Margaret Fuller have admired his fiction;[4] and
critics generally agree that the best of Brown's novels show his
great, but unrealized, talent. Admittedly, all of his books contain
serious flaws, yet they have their strengths as well. The breathless pace of the best of his narratives, the taut suspense he was
able at times to maintain, the sense of immediacy he could instill
in some of his episodes, the convincing depiction of abnormal
mental states, the verisimilitude of the scenes that are laid in
plague-ridden Philadelphia—all are elements worthy of critical
praise. They go a long way, moreover, in helping to mitigate the
glaring faults in plotting, characterization, and style that would
surely destroy the artistic effect entirely, if his books did not also
generate such utterly absorbing interest. Brown's novels cannot
be dismissed, therefore, as having only historical importance. The
best of them still live; and, as a number of critics have testified,
they can yet be read for their real—if limited—literary value.

Although there is general agreement upon the importance and
worth of Brown's achievement, opinion is curiously divided about
the relative merits of individual books and the general thematic
meaning of his fiction. Each of the major novels, for example,
has had its defenders. *Wieland,* of course, is generally considered
to be the most successful, and *Edgar Huntly* is usually ranked
second. Yet George Snell believes that *Arthur Mervyn* is best and
dismisses the whole framework of *Edgar Huntly* as "entirely

incredible."[5] Leslie A. Fiedler, on the other hand, considers *Edgar Huntly* "the most successful and characteristic of his gothic romances,"[6] and Martin S. Vilas puts *Ormond* forward as Brown's "best work."[7]

Opinion is similarly divided on the meaning of Brown's themes. David Lee Clark argues, for example, that Brown's purpose in his novels was to disseminate the radical thought that swept through Europe toward the close of the eighteenth century,[8] but Alexander Cowie writes that Brown includes in his fiction "radical doctrine which he did not necessarily endorse."[9] Moreover, a recent critic of *Wieland*, Larzer Ziff, finds Brown in that book presenting a view that is precisely the opposite of what Lewis observes in *Arthur Mervyn*.[10]

Such a degree of critical confusion can be explained in a number of ways. Part undoubtedly derives from the fact that Brown never wrote a completely satisfactory novel. Since all of his works are imperfect, each is likely to be valued for a different reason, and one is chosen over another because of the critical predilection of the reader. One whose taste runs toward the realistic might well prefer the plague scenes of *Arthur Mervyn* to everything else that Brown wrote, but another whose primary interest lies in the psychological state of the characters will probably value *Wieland* or *Edgar Huntly* the highest. Disagreements of this sort can never be resolved, for they are caused by inevitable differences in taste. Others, however, deriving from a misjudgment of Brown or a misinterpretation of his novels can surely be settled by an examination of his background and a thorough analysis of his books. The view, for example, that Brown was the strong proponent of contemporary radical thought who wrote his novels to disseminate such doctrine must certainly be rejected if it can be shown that the themes of his books run sharply counter to much of that thought, or that Brown himself was a far more complex person than this view might suggest.

Any interpretation of Brown, therefore, that seeks to resolve the critical disagreement his works have engendered must first go back to the man himself, his intellectual background and development, and concentrate finally on close analysis of his literary work. The initial stress on biography is inevitable, for the study of Brown's early life is most pertinent to the discussion of his art. Charles Brockden Brown put much of himself into his books. This is not to say that they are autobiographical in any strict sense of the word, or that Brown should be identified with any of the characters through whom he projects his themes. The relation, one suspects, is far more subtle than that. An intellectually alert young man, Brown was much concerned with ideas, and there can be no question that he was deeply interested in the ones he expressed in his books. Indeed, two of his ablest critics—Harry R. Warfel and R. W. B. Lewis—see an even more intimate relation between Brown's life and work, for both suggest that writing was for him a kind of therapy through which he came to grips with the problems that troubled him.[11] Be that as it may—and the suggestion is an alluring one—a review of Brown's early life is clearly in order.

II *Personal Background*

Born to Quaker parents in Philadelphia on January 17, 1771, Charles Brockden Brown grew up a rather frail, bookish young man. He attended the Friends' Latin School, conducted by Robert Proud, until about his sixteenth year; and, instead of going to college—higher education was generally frowned upon by Quakers—he was apprenticed to Alexander Wilcocks to study law. Brown, however, was already developing an interest in things literary. He planned three epic poems on the discovery of America and the conquests of Mexico and Peru, and he joined with a group of young men to form the Belles Lettres Club, the purpose of which was to improve the members' skill in writing and eloquence. Although Brown continued to study law until not long after his twenty-first birthday,[12] he never practiced his profession; he argued with his family that he could not bring himself, on moral grounds, to become a defender of injustice or an advocate for a wrong cause. His family, though grieved, finally accepted his decision and allowed him freedom to pursue a literary career, probably because, as Warfel has observed, his health at this time fell into decline and he sank into one of his severe—and recurring—melancholy moods (37-38).

More important, however, from the point of view of his subsequent literary career are the intellectual influences that he came under. The most significant one, no doubt, was his parents' Quakerism, which surely gave his mind the liberal bent that was to develop so strongly during his early manhood.[13] His wide but undisciplined reading, moreover, undoubtedly confirmed this inclination, and he surely absorbed the revolutionary doctrine so much in the air in Philadelphia during his youth. As his modern biographers attest, he was quite familiar with much contemporary thought even before he came under the influence of Godwin's *Political Justice* and *Caleb Williams* during the 1790's.[14] Since his father, too, although a devout Quaker, read such books as *Political Justice*, Mary Wollstonecraft's *French Revolution*, and Robert Bage's *Man As He Is* when they appeared,[15] it seems fair to assume that Brockden Brown grew up in a family generally conversant with contemporary ideas. Further influence toward radicalism, moreover, came without question from his close friendship with Elihu Hubbard Smith, a young deist and physician who arrived in Philadelphia in September, 1790, to study medicine, and who was also strongly influenced by the radical thought of the times.

The friendship begun here was to continue until the untimely death of Smith in New York during the yellow fever epidemic of 1798. Brown paid a number of visits to his new friend, first in Connecticut in 1793, and later in New York, where, in 1794, he became acquainted with members of the Friendly Club, to which Smith belonged. Brown attended meetings of this society when visiting Smith and his other friends in that city. Here he could take part in serious conversation on important issues of the day with the group of young Federalists who made up its membership.[16] Among these men, moreover, was William Dunlap—playwright, painter, eventual historian of both American art and American drama, and biographer of Brown—who, with Smith, became an intimate friend of the young Philadelphian. Brockden Brown was thus caught up in some of the intellectual current of the times, and he made the most of the experience. It was with Smith's and Dunlap's encouragement that Brown attempted to launch his literary career, and Smith in particular gave the greatest help of all by actually publishing Brown's initial book, Parts I and II of *Alcuin,* a dialogue on the rights of women.

Although *Alcuin* is, from the point of view of literary value, a rather poor book, it remains of interest not only as the first major publication of America's earliest professional novelist, but more especially as an insight into Brown's mind in 1797, when it probably was written.[17] As such, it clearly reveals the liberal bent which his background and reading had given it. In the dialogue between Alcuin, a poor schoolmaster, and Mrs. Carter, a widow and "bluestocking"—neither of whom is at all well depicted—Brown expresses some extremely liberal views for his time. Thus, Parts I and II, published by Smith, suggest the need for a sounder education for women so that they may play a more useful and independent role in society, and include an argument by Mrs. Carter for political equality with men. In the third and fourth parts, moreover, most likely suppressed by Smith and not printed until they were included in Dunlap's *Life* in 1815,[18] Brown airs ideas which are even more radical. He allows Alcuin to portray a visionary society in which all social differences between the sexes have been obliterated and marriage is unheard of; and, although he has Mrs. Carter defend the institution of marriage, Brown ends with her stating an opinion in support of divorce.

Yet despite the radical ideas that Brown presents through the characters in *Alcuin*, we cannot assume that he remained for long an extremist in his own opinions. That he tended to skepticism we know on Dunlap's authority, but his friend and biographer also observed, in apology for the views presented in *Alcuin*, that "much of [Brown's] reading at this time tended to bewilder rather than enlighten" him so that he attributed the defects of the world to the wrong causes, the codes by which men live, rather than "to the ignorance and selfishness of individuals."[19] Such a view, of course, would be generally in accord with the radical ideas we know he acquired from his reading. Dunlap goes on to say, however, that the "plunging tenets and dangerous doctrines" which he expressed in *Alcuin* gradually changed as he mingled in society and observed the manners of men (I, 71); and he finally came to adopt a more conservative view. Though we cannot trace in any detail the evolution of his thought, there is considerable evidence to suggest that, although Brown was always fascinated with Utopian schemes and even sketched Utopian plans himself,[20] he turned away from actual acceptance of them by the time he wrote his novels.

Even in *Alcuin*, for example, Brown is careful not to go to extremes with his views. Although he generally allows Mrs. Carter to espouse liberal causes, she does interrupt the schoolmaster's description of the visionary society to express her disapproval of those thinkers who, in her own words, "aim at the deepest foundation of civil society."[21] Indeed, in all of the novels which followed that book into print, Brown never lends his

assent to Utopian schemes. It is always the villainous characters—
Carwin, Ludloe, and Ormond—who are most strongly influenced
by radical thought; and their actions are, without exception,
productive of a multitude of evils against which the virtuous
characters are forced to struggle. The entire action of *Ormond,*
moreover, opposes many of the radical ideas that Brown had
picked up in his reading.[22] In the light of such evidence, one is
reluctant to believe that Brown remained himself the proponent
of such ideas. That they held an interest for him cannot be
doubted. But it seems most reasonable to assume that he used
them in his fiction for artistic rather than for propagandistic
purposes.

To stress unduly the rationalist side of Brown's personality
may lead to a serious misunderstanding of the man and his work,
for there was an element in his make-up that points in quite a
different direction. For years Brown seems to have been afflicted
with a strange emotional disorder, perhaps derived in part from
his poor physical health. He fell into spells of melancholy that
can only be called abnormal, and his letters reveal the depths of
morbid self-criticism into which he sometimes slipped. Joseph
Brown had apparently recognized this trait in his younger
brother, because he stressed in his letters to him the importance
of keeping one's "fears and anxieties" from the eyes of others.[23]

Brown attempted to heed his brother's advice, but he was not
entirely successful. Although he does not reveal much about
himself that is really specific even in letters to his closest friends,
his reticence is not complete. Rather, he sometimes hints darkly
at unspeakable mysteries. Thus, in a letter to his friend William
W. Wilkins—the very letter, indeed, in which he reveals his
brother's advice—Brown wrote: "what useful purpose could be
answered by making C. B. B. better known to his friends? What
but their unhappiness could be produced by it?" Indeed, he even
writes of "that profound abyss of ignominy and debasement, into
which I am sunk by my own reflections."[24]

Smith and Dunlap, too, received such letters from their friend,
and Smith in particular wrote two long replies in May, 1796, in
which, playing the psychologist, he tries to talk Brown out of
his strange affliction. He berates him soundly for being neither
wholly reticent nor completely explicit in his self-revelation, and
he attempts to bring his friend into a more healthy mental state.[25]
His advice, however, seems to have done little permanent good,

because nearly two years later, on January 1, 1798, Brown expressed, in a letter to Dunlap, such extremes of morbid self-consciousness and depths of self-abhorrence that Dunlap did not acknowledge it; he merely wrote on the manuscript his expression of regret that his beloved friend could sometimes write in such a manner.[26] The point, of course, must not be overstressed, for Brown should no more be viewed as a mental case than he should be seen as an utter rationalist. The evidence is important, nonetheless, in helping the critic to a balanced view of the man and in suggesting a possible source in Brown himself for that interest in human psychology so apparent in his fiction.

Charles Brockden Brown, it seems fair to conclude, was a complex person who cannot be simply or easily characterized. Intelligent, alert, greatly interested in contemporary ideas, he was also a man frequently ill in body and deeply troubled in mind. His very complexity, moreover, must surely have had an effect on his writing; and, as one reads through the novels, he is increasingly drawn to the suggestion that they did indeed serve a therapeutic purpose for him—if not in curing his melancholy, at least in helping him clarify his thought. For Brown's views underwent a dramatic change during the course of a relatively few years. Obviously influenced by the rationalist thought of Godwin and others during the early stage of his career, Brown made his first attempt at novel writing in 1795 with what was presumably an imitation of *Caleb Williams*,[27] and he published in *Alcuin* views that were certainly radical for his time. Yet in his final novel, *Jane Talbot*, published in 1801, Brown presents a much more conservative view. He specifically opposes Godwinian rationalism and affirms the value of religious faith as the guide to life. Though we cannot assume, of course, that Brown rejected entirely all he had read in his youth, the evidence clearly reveals that he changed his opinions considerably during the period of his intense artistic creation; and one is drawn to the view that, to some extent, the writing itself helped him to formulate his final intellectual position.

III *Fictional Method*

Such an interpretation gains support from the manner in which the novels were written. We have it on Dunlap's authority that Brown did not make in advance an overall plan for a book, but developed its form as he wrote: "He began to write a novel after having only determined upon one leading circumstance, character or idea, and trusted to the growth of one incident from another, and the appropriate sentiments from the incidents. One volume would be finished and printed before he had formed any plan for the beginning of the second, or any plan for the continuation, developement or denouement of the story" (I, 258).

What happened in the process is well illustrated by the second part of *Arthur Mervyn*. Brown, we know, had made at least a general plan for the book before he began to write;[28] but he made some major changes as the work progressed. The character of Mrs. Achsa Fielding is not even mentioned in his original statement, yet she is the woman whom Mervyn eventually marries in the completed novel! Because of her presence, the story comes to a conclusion significantly different in meaning from what Brown had apparently first intended, a meaning which could only have developed while Brown was composing the book.[29]

A recent analysis of Brown's fictional method lends further weight to the hypothesis that Brown developed his themes in the course of the writing itself. For W. B. Berthoff has observed, in an important article, that Brown did not use narration merely to illustrate preconceived ideas; he made it, rather, "an instrument for *discovering* ideas, for exploring and testing them out." Thus, Berthoff argues, Brown did not set out to expound ideas in his books—not Godwin's, nor, indeed, his own—but put them to the test of action by contriving incidents in which the characters attempt to live by the concepts and put them into practice. Through a series of such incidents, each of which restates or deepens the central idea, a theme emerges which may be something quite different from the concepts explicitly stated in the book. The theme arises, therefore, from the total action of the story, and, at times, seems to defy simple expression because it takes cognizance of the conflicts and contradictions in human nature and reflects the full complexity of human experience.[30]

It should be apparent, therefore, that the critic of Brown who hopes to arrive at a valid interpretation of the novels and at a just estimate of their literary worth must lay his preconceptions aside and turn his attention to the close analysis of the individual books. The task, of course, is complicated by a number of factors. Since the novels took form as he wrote them and probably did not develop according to any preconceived plan, the reader is presented with obvious difficulties that are only compounded by the complex order of composition of the books themselves. According to Dunlap, Brown at one time had five novels going at once (II, 16), and there is no way now to determine the precise order of their development. *Arthur Mervyn*, for example, may have been begun as early as 1795, and the first nine chapters of it preceded *Wieland* in print, yet it stands in the order of publication as Brown's third novel. In a similar fashion, *Edgar Huntly* appeared as his fourth, but parts of it probably derive from his earliest and now lost novel, *Sky-Walk; or, The Man Unknown to Himself,* finished late in 1797.[31] Indeed, Brown sometimes even borrowed from his own writings, for the same or similar episodes occasionally appear in more than one work.[32]

Fortunately, however, the problem of chronological order need not concern us unduly, for Brown's career as a novelist—or at least the major part of it—was much too short to make the order of composition of overriding importance. Besides, there are other problems that demand our critical attention. In some important ways, Brown's fictional techniques foreshadow the devices of the modern novelist, and questions of interpretation in his books are sometimes those that we are familiar with from more recent fiction. The first-person method of narration by which most of his books are developed and the multiple point of view he employed in *Wieland* and in *Arthur Mervyn* are cases in point. Although the devices certainly add to the interest of the novels, the complications of meaning that sometimes arise from their use make the books, like many modern ones, somewhat difficult to analyze. The reader, however, should not be deterred for that reason. The problem of interpretation can become an absorbing one, and the rewards to be obtained are substantial. Brown's books, at their best, contain much of artistic value; and, even at their worst, they add considerably to our understanding of many important developments in subsequent American fiction.

CHAPTER 2

Wieland

THE PUBLICATION of *Wieland; or, The Transformation* in the late summer of 1798 marks the true beginning of Brown's literary career; for, although he had already written both *Alcuin* and *Sky-Walk* and had published a number of minor pieces,[1] *Wieland* is the first of his major works to be published in its entirety. The book appeared in September[2] at the height of the yellow fever epidemic which had struck New York in August and which, before it had run its course, was to strike down his friend, Elihu Hubbard Smith, and force Brown himself, who was living in New York at the time and had contracted the disease, to move to Perth Amboy, New Jersey. Despite the unfortunate timing of the publication, however, the book seems to have been reasonably well received. The few reviews that appeared after the subsidence of the plague recognized the novel as a superior one—the best, certainly, that had yet appeared in America.[3] Subsequent criticism has generally supported this opinion: *Wieland* continues to be regarded as the first truly significant novel by an American and as the most successful work of its author. Its virtues, indeed, are many. The breathless, headlong style, the suspenseful main plot, and the inexorable movement of the action to its dénouement certainly mark its relative success, despite some considerable faults, as a work of art.

I *The Problem of Interpretation*

Although the book has been justly praised, relatively little attention has been paid, until quite recently, to an explication of its meaning. The older critics, in general, approached the book historically. Fred Lewis Pattee, for example, points out the strong influence of eighteenth-century English fiction on the novel;[4] and David Lee Clark has observed that Brown goes beyond the Gothic tale of horror and the sentimental novel of seduction, both of which left their mark on his work, to adopt "the principles of the Novel of Purpose, made prominent by Holcroft, Bage, and Godwin" (164-65). Although studies like these have placed the book in the proper historical context, their approach to the work incurs the serious danger of misinterpretation, as is well illustrated by Clark's analysis of the novel. Aware of the impact of eighteenth-century philosophy on the young Brown, Clark treats the book as an exposition of radical thought. In his view, *Wieland* becomes "a sermon against credulity and religious fanaticism" (168-69), and he discusses the book primarily in these terms.

This interpretation, of course, is made plausible by certain factors in the novel: the character of Theodore Wieland, whose religious mania transforms him into a madman who kills his wife and children, and the statement of purpose that his sister Clara makes in the opening pages of the novel. Clara informs the reader that the book "will exemplify the force of early impressions, and show the immeasurable evils that flow from an erroneous or imperfect discipline" (I, 25)—a view which seems to imply that the novel will merely present a rationalist concept. When one considers as well that Wieland's mania is strongly influenced by the early impressions he received at the mysterious death of his father, the attractiveness of the interpretation becomes apparent. Yet such a view seriously oversimplifies the meaning of the book. It assumes that Wieland is the central character, and it leaves generally out of account any important consideration of the function served by the other major characters: Wieland's sister, Clara; his brother-in-law, Pleyel; and the villainous Carwin—all of whose thoughts and actions contribute significantly to the meaning of the tale.

One might better assume, with Warfel, that the central character is Clara (106-7);[5] for it is she, not Wieland, who is the focal point of the action—and it is she and Pleyel, not Wieland, as Clark erroneously asserts (166), who are the targets of Carwin's evil machinations. Wieland, moreover, is not the only character to undergo a transformation during the course of the story; for Clara and Pleyel too are transformed by their experience. Wieland is thus only one of several characters through whom the theme is projected, and it can be argued that his experience is by no means the most significant. Any interpreta-

tion, therefore, which places primary stress on Wieland is likely
to distort the meaning of the book. To arrive at a valid interpretation, it is better to lay aside historical preconceptions and carefully analyze the novel itself to determine the function of all the
characters in presenting the theme. By approaching the book in
this way, the critic soon finds that the meaning of *Wieland* is
something quite different from what has sometimes been
supposed.

This is not to deny, of course, that the book contains substantial evidence of Brown's knowledge and understanding of many
contemporary ideas—or to minimize their importance in interpreting the novel. Indeed, the whole action of the book is based
upon the sensationalist psychology of the time.[6] The characters
repeatedly stress their belief in its validity, and Clara herself
summarizes its basic tenets succinctly when she asserts: "The
will is the tool of the understanding, which must fashion its conclusions on the notices of sense" (I, 55). In other words, they
accept in general the view that man is the passive recipient of
sensory impressions and that from these data alone he derives
the knowledge on which he bases all thought and action.[7] But
to show that Brown made use of sensationalist psychology in his
book does not necessarily mean that he accepted it uncritically,
for the developing action of the novel calls its validity into serious
question.[8] From beginning to end, the characters are chiefly
concerned with the problem of discerning the truth that lies
behind the appearance of things in the world; and the action
consistently shows the difficulty they experience in drawing
just inferences from the evidence of their senses.

Brown's method in developing the book is that which Berthoff
describes as his usual one.[9] The characters act in a series of anal-
ogous incidents that test the ideas by which they attempt to live,
and the cumulative effect clearly reveals the central theme. In
Wieland, Brown creates a number of attractive and "enlightened"
young people whose thoughts and actions, when they are confronted by unusual circumstances, unmistakably demonstrate the
fundamental meaning of the book. The group centers around the
Wieland family: Theodore, a studious young man with a certain
Calvinistic streak in his intellectual make-up; his wife, Catherine;
and their four children. Clara Wieland, who idolizes her brother
and has shared his education, lives but a short distance away and
is constantly in their company. A fourth member of the group is

Catherine's brother, Henry Pleyel, a gay young rationalist who frequently comes to visit them. The Wielands live an almost idyllic existence in semi-rural isolation on the banks of the Schuylkill, but there is an important element in their past from the influence of which they can never escape, and an unexpected and unforeseen future waits to test them severely.

II *Background to the Action*

Always in the background lies the history of the elder Wieland, the father of Theodore and Clara. The son of a disinherited German nobleman, he is apprenticed to a London merchant, who works him long and hard. Somewhat morose and given to gloomy reflection, he is haunted by a nameless craving that is only satisfied when he chances upon a religious book and finds a theme for meditation. Guided by the Camisard tract he has read, he becomes increasingly introspective, constructs a private religion of his own, develops an intensely scrupulous conscience, and labors "to keep alive a sentiment of fear, and a belief of the awe-creating presence of the Deity" (I, 29). Convinced that he must disseminate his belief, he journeys to America to preach it to the Indians, a mission he tries to perform only after he has successfully established himself in the country for fourteen years. Failing in his missionary task, however, he retires to his farm on the Schuylkill and increasingly isolates himself from men. He avoids all forms of social worship and even constructs a kind of temple "on the top of a rock whose sides were steep, rugged, and encumbered with dwarf cedars and stony asperities" where, in a space that was "without seat, table, or ornament of any kind," he worships his God alone each day at midnight and noon (I, 31). He comes to believe, however, that he has failed to obey a command laid on him and that his offense is inexpiable. Foreseeing his approaching end, he goes alone to his temple at midnight. An eerie light appears; he is struck a heavy blow; his clothes are burned to ashes; and, after falling into fever, delirium, and a lethargic sleep, he later dies.

Clara is a child of six at the time, her brother apparently slightly older; and the death of their father by such mysterious means has a lasting effect on them. Clara, in particular, writing many years after the event, still cannot decide whether the death is to be assigned a supernatural or a natural cause—whether her father died by the direct stroke of the divine hand, or, as Brown suggests, of the "natural" cause of spontaneous combustion.[10] In any event, the occurrence lingers in their memories to reappear at times of crisis throughout the book, even though to all external appearances the young people have tried to put their strange parent and his mysterious death behind them.

Orphaned by the early death of their mother, the children are raised in accordance with "enlightened" principles. "By accident more than design," the maiden aunt who educates them mingles the proper amounts of indulgence and steadfastness in forming their characters, sees that they are properly instructed "in most branches of useful knowledge," but preserves them "from the corruption and tyranny of colleges and boarding-schools" (I, 40). Even the temple is reclaimed from its previous use. Wieland places a bust of Cicero and a harpsichord in the place where his father worshiped, and the group retires there on summer evenings to sing, talk, read, and occasionally banquet.

Their attitude toward religion is, of course, much different from what their father's had been. Their "education had been modelled by no religious standard," for they were "left to the guidance of [their] own understanding and the casual impressions which society might make upon [them]." Clara and Catherine are not without religious sentiment, but with them it is only "the product of lively feelings, excited by reflection on [their] own happiness, and by the grandeur of external nature" (I, 42). Wieland, however, is somewhat different. More deeply religious than his sister, he nonetheless attempts to find an intellectual basis for his belief: "He was much conversant with the history of religious opinions, and took pains to ascertain their validity. He deemed it indispensable to examine the ground of his belief, to settle the relation between motives and actions, the criterion of merit, and the kinds and properties of evidence." Though obviously resembling his father in his concern with religion, "the mind of the son," Clara glibly tells us, "was enriched by science and embellished with literature" (I, 43). Children of their age, they accept most of its assumptions and settle down to several pleasant years in their retreat.

Their retired society, moreover, is made all the more pleasurable by the addition of the gay Pleyel, a man whose "discernment was acute" but who "was prone to view every object merely as supplying materials for mirth." As well educated as Wieland, he is "not behind his friend in his knowledge of the history and metaphysics of religion." But Wieland is fundamentally a believer, and Pleyel is a complete rationalist. "The champion of intellectual liberty," he rejects "all guidance but that of his reason" (I, 44-45) and denies faith "to any testimony but that of his senses" (I, 94). In Pleyel, therefore, we have the "enlightened" man in test-tube purity, but he is not so different from Wieland that the two cannot get along. They frequently discuss their differences of opinion and manage their arguments with candor and skill. Indeed, their fundamental attitudes toward knowledge are not really so diverse as one might expect. Both are concerned with the analysis and evaluation of the available evidence. Their difference lies in their conclusions; for, "where one discovered only confirmations of his faith, the other could find nothing but reasons for doubt" (I, 45). Their arguments are thus entirely friendly and do not detract at all from the pleasure each enjoys in the other's company.

The Wielands' pleasant life is suddenly disrupted, however, when Brown introduces an element designed to put the characters' views to a serious test. One night, after a sudden shower drives the group from the temple, Wieland returns alone to pick up a letter inadvertently left there. He hears a voice which sounds like his wife's call out to him to stop because there is danger before him and to return to the house. Since the voice is heard under circumstances which make it impossible for it to have been Catherine's, Wieland is faced with the difficulty of drawing an inference from unaccountable sense impressions. Wieland, however, is not alone with this problem. Some three weeks later, as he and Pleyel talk alone in the temple at night, the rationalist Pleyel, who had dismissed the first voice as an illusion of the senses, hears it too and is forced to admit its reality. Clara too is eventually confronted with the phenomenon, for, still later, she hears mysterious voices whispering in her room late at night; and the whole household, finally, is awakened by a strange call, when Clara, fleeing the voices in her room, faints at her brother's doorstep. All the characters, therefore, are compelled to interpret sense impressions which seem to have no easily discernible basis in reality and which are at the very least ambiguous. By this means, Brown initiates the series of experiences which form the basic structure of the book and through which is revealed its central theme.

Clara's words and actions before he heard the voices. The thoroughness of his delusion, therefore, clearly reveals the serious error in the rationalist theory by which Pleyel has attempted to live—its failure to take sufficiently into account that all men, no matter how rational, possess fallible minds and powerful passions. Though he admits "the limitedness of human faculties" (I, 140), Pleyel seems unable to recognize his own fallibility when he succumbs to his passions.[11]

It is small wonder, then, that Wieland too fails at solving the problem, since he is influenced by far more sinister forces than any with which the less complex Pleyel has had to contend. The memory of his father's death forever lurks in his mind and always comes to the fore whenever he visits the temple alone or at night. It is thus already present on that fateful evening when Carwin first projects his imitation of Catherine's voice. The effect is immediate and profound. Always a grave and thoughtful person, Wieland becomes even more introspective after that experience; and his thoughts, thereafter, "were generally found to have a relation more or less direct with this incident." Since he had always considered his father's death as "flowing from a direct and supernatural decree" (I, 55), it is not difficult for him to believe that the voice he has heard may derive from a supernatural source—a conclusion which predisposes him to hear additional commands. Hence, when later voices, not produced by Carwin, urge him to monstrous acts against his wife and children, Wieland, crossing the line between sanity and madness, obeys what he thinks is a divine command in killing them.

Yet Wieland is not so different from Pleyel as his madness might seem to indicate, for he is no less certain of his ability to arrive at truth through the interpretation of sensory evidence. When Pleyel tells him of his belief in Clara's guilt, Wieland does not think it possible for Pleyel to have been deceived. Nonetheless, he is willing to accept Clara's vindication of herself but only because long experience has attested to her veracity, and "nothing less than [his] own hearing and vision would convince [him], in opposition to her own assertions, that [his] sister had fallen into wickedness like this" (I, 128-29). That he should refer to his senses in this way is ironic in view of Pleyel's error,[12] but Wieland is consistent in his acceptance of sensory evidence; and, even in his homicidal mania, he believes he is acting as a perfectly reasonable man. Thus, when he recounts the events of the night on which he hears the voice order him to kill his wife, he describes the sequence rationally as a simple association of ideas. The happiness he feels in his love for his wife and children fills him with thoughts of gratitude to God, from whom his blessings flow, and gratitude leads him to thoughts of the service due so great a benefactor.

In a moment of exaltation, then, Wieland longs for "the blissful privilege of direct communication with [God], and of listening to the audible enunciation of [His] pleasure"; and he prays: "Would that a momentary emanation from thy glory would visit me! that some unambiguous token of thy presence would salute my senses!" (I, 185-86). When he sees the vision and hears the voice which, shortly thereafter, commands him to kill his wife, he accepts what he sees and hears as valid sensory evidence. That this and the subsequent voices exist in his mind alone is clearly underscored in the book, but the point of the matter is that they seem real to him, that he is thoroughly convinced of their objectivity. With Wieland, therefore, Brown is ringing a variation on the theme which he developed in the character of Pleyel. The rationalist fails in interpreting true sensations accurately, but his friend is unable to distinguish between true and false sensations.

The implications of Wieland's experience, moreover, may have an even greater significance than is at first apparent, for Larzer Ziff has argued that it makes the most telling comment on the optimistic psychology that informs the book. Whereas Pleyel's errors may be dismissed as simply a temporary delusion of the individual, Wieland's suggest, in Ziff's analysis, a much more fundamental flaw in his condition. Early in the novel, after Wieland first hears what he thinks is Catherine's voice warning him from the temple, Clara analyzes the problem and states the question explicitly. She does not like to think that Wieland has suffered a delusion because it argues "a diseased condition of his frame, which might show itself hereafter in more dangerous symptoms. The will is the tool of the understanding, which must fashion its conclusions on the notices of sense. If the senses be depraved, it is impossible to calculate the evils that may flow from the consequent deductions of the understanding" (I, 55). *Depraved*, Ziff believes, is the key word in the passage, for it implies that human nature is not so simple as contemporary psychology would have it. Wieland has, most likely, inherited his mania from his father. In Ziff's opinion, therefore, Wieland succumbs not to a simple delusion of the senses but to "an inherited depravity which preceded it," a view of human nature which, with its strong Calvinistic overtones, runs counter to the optimistic psychology of the day (53-54).

IV *A Major Variation*

Be that as it may, Brown's exploration of the problem does not end at this point. Yet another—and major—variation on the theme is provided by Clara's experience. Although she resembles both Pleyel and Wieland in some of her mental attitudes, Clara is in many ways quite different from both. Like Pleyel, of course, she accepts the psychology of the time; but, although she is generally averse to any supernatural explanation of strange events, she does eventually come to believe that the voices they hear are from a benevolent supernatural source. Like Wieland, moreover, she feels the strong influence of the past in the recurring memory of her father's death and even recognizes in herself "an hereditary dread of water" (I, 101). But, unlike her brother, she engages in no brooding thoughts on religious matters and professes only a rather vague, liberal religion, "the product of lively feelings"; and she seeks no "basis for [her] faith in the weighing of proofs and the dissection of creeds" (I, 42). Deeply involved with problems in psychology, however, Clara seeks causes and explanations of all the strange phenomena which occur and ponders much on the problem of interpreting conflicting and ambiguous sensations. In the course of her musings, she stumbles upon some phenomena for which she cannot rationally account.[13]

This process begins shortly after the appearance of Carwin, whom Clara first sees when he stops at the house to ask for a drink to quench his thirst. Impressed by the mellifluous voice which she hears, she is surprised to find, when she sees his face, that he is strangely ugly. There are about him, however, signs that "betoken a mind of the highest order" (I, 73). Unaccountably affected by the appearance of the man, she sketches his portrait; and, sitting alone in her apartment the following dark and stormy day, she gazes at it until her mind becomes "absorbed in thoughts ominous and dreary." Even when she turns fondly to the images of her brother and his children, "they only increased the mournfulness of [her] contemplations." The smiles of the children are as bland as ever and the brow of the father as dignified, but for some inexplicable reason she thinks of them "with anguish" (I, 74). As yet, nothing has occurred to connect the mysterious Carwin with any of the unusual events. Indeed, she has seen him only briefly and has not yet spoken to him at all. Yet, somehow, her mind has made a connection between the curious stranger and her own beloved family.

This incident is not the only instance of a strange process in Clara's mind. Some weeks later, after "a toilsome day," Clara goes alone to her summerhouse on the bank of the river to recoup her spirits depressed "through the fatigue of long attention." "The lulling sounds of the waterfall," the fragrance of the honeysuckle, and the gathering dusk of evening succeed in becalming her spirits; and in a short time she falls asleep. Her dreams, however, are anything but peaceful. After some incoherent episodes, she finds herself, in the twilight of evening, approaching her brother's house, unaware of a pit that lay in her path. "As I carelessly pursued my walk," she writes, "I thought I saw my brother standing at some distance before me, beckoning and calling me to make haste. He stood on the opposite edge of the gulf. I mended my pace, and one step more would have plunged me into this abyss, had not some one from behind caught suddenly my arm, and exclaimed, in a voice of eagerness and terror, 'Hold! hold!'" (I, 81-82). Clara suddenly starts awake only to hear a mysterious voice warn her away from that spot. Elsewhere, it informs her, she will be safe, but here the danger of death awaits her.

Clara, of course, is seriously affected by this incident and ponders over it long. Since she accepts the evidence of her senses when she knows she is fully awake, she considers the warning to have been a valid one; but she and the reader later learn that it was merely Carwin trying to frighten her away from the summerhouse, where he is carrying on an affair with her servant, Judith. She dismisses the dream, on the other hand, as purely imaginary, as a mere phantom (I, 105), when in reality it forewarns her of a danger that does indeed impend. The rationalist in Clara, however, does not accept the dream as anything but a fantasy, and she finds it impossible to explain the ideas that subsequently well up in her mind. The following month, after Pleyel, whom she loves, has failed to appear for an appointed rehearsal of a new German play, she fears some accident may have befallen him, and she sits in her room that

night musing upon the dangers and cares of human life. Recall-
ing by association, then, her father's terrible end, she decides
to read in the memoirs of his life that he had left in manuscript.
She starts to her closet to get it, unaware that Carwin is trapped
inside; but, remembering the whispered voices she had heard
coming from that room a number of weeks before, she is suddenly filled with fear. Her mind darts to the conclusion that some
being with evil intent lies concealed within (I, 103).

From this point on, Clara's mind receives a series of powerful shocks, and she finds herself unable to account for the mental
process that results. Her faith in the validity of her sensations is
shaken when, hearing a voice that seems to come from behind
her and that warns her away from the door, she looks about the
room but sees nothing. "Which of my senses," she asks, "was the
prey of a fatal illusion?" (I, 104). That she heard the sound
cannot be doubted, yet the person who seemed to be standing
at her right ear when he spoke is nowhere to be seen. She begins
to wonder, too, at the strange parallel between her present experience and her frightening dream in the summerhouse. On the
night of her dream, she was made aware "by some inexplicable
contrivance" of the danger that impended. Yet, she writes, "my
actions and sensations were those of one wholly unacquainted
with it. Now, was it not equally true that my actions and per-
suasions were at war? Had not the belief that evil lurked in the
closet gained admittance, and had not my actions betokened an
unwarrantable security?" (I, 105). Clara is deeply disturbed by
the strange relation that seems to exist between the danger she
perceives and the way she reacts when she learns of it, and by
the similar voices that have warned her of her peril.

As she ponders the problem, moreover, Clara arrives at a conclusion which, although unsupported by any reasonable evidence
and wrong in the immediate incident, is nonetheless essentially
right in pinpointing both the person she should fear and the
danger that threatens. Since the voice that warns her now away
from the closet recalls the one that saved her in her dream, and
since it saved her then from her brother, who seemed to beckon
her to destruction, she becomes convinced that it is Wieland who
lurks in the closet and that he intends to kill her. Clara struggles
against this idea as a "strange and terrible chimera," but it will
not be dismissed. She concludes, therefore, that "it was surely no
vulgar agency that gave this form to [her] fears. He to whom all

parts of time are equally present, whom no contingency approaches, was the author of that spell which had seized upon [her]." Yet, even though she believes that an omen of her fate has been communicated to her in her dream, she cannot understand why she does not flee the evil that approaches. Indeed, she actually rushes to meet it; for, in her strange infatuation, she tries to force the closet door and calls on him within to come out. It is small wonder, then, that Clara concludes from her experience: "Ideas exist in our minds that can be accounted for by no established laws" (I, 106-7).

That Brown expects the reader to entertain this conclusion seriously is apparent from the ensuing action, because he makes no attempt to explain away Clara's dream or the strange thoughts and actions that follow it. Subsequent events, in fact, only confirm her prophetic fears; for, once Wieland has killed his wife and children, his imagined voices demand the death of Clara as well; and, three times escaping from prison to pursue her, he makes several violent attempts on her life. When Clara finally learns, moreover, that Wieland in his madness has sought to kill her, she recalls her dream. "I recollected the omens of this destiny," she writes; "I remembered the gulf to which my brother's invitation had conducted me; I remembered that, when on the brink of danger, the author of my peril was depicted by my fears in his form. Thus realized were the creatures of prophetic sleep and of wakeful terror" (I, 208-9). Indeed, the dream is prophetic in yet another sense. When Wieland is on the point of killing her at the climax of the book, he is stopped by the same voice, Carwin's, and by the same command that had saved her in the dream (I, 248).

Clara, of course, is almost destroyed by all that happens, for the very foundations of her life have been swept away from her. She comes to question the validity of her sensations and to doubt her ability to act in accordance with their promptings. Her mind leaps to conclusions for which there is no sensory evidence, but subsequent events confirm their truth. She finds herself reviled by Pleyel on the basis of valid if misinterpreted sensations, and she sees her brother fall victim to an inherited mania that makes him a prey to illusory sense impressions. Her mind is unstrung at the deaths of Catherine and the children; and, after her final encounter with the maniacal Wieland, she goes completely mad. Clara is eventually reclaimed, of course, when her rationalist uncle takes her to Europe; she eventually marries Pleyel, after Carwin has disabused him of his error; and she ends by moralizing on her terrible experience. Yet the conventional happy ending of the book rings false and should not be allowed to obscure the more serious conclusion toward which the main action of the novel had been tending: that human beings are much more complex than the contemporary psychology assumed and that their motives and actions are not so simply explained.[14]

V *Further Ramifications*

Other ramifications of the problem, moreover, are developed in the book. Brown could not call into question the validity of the optimistic psychology of the day without undercutting as well the whole rationalist view of man and society that ultimately is based upon it. Such a conclusion is certainly supported by the character of Carwin, the villain who precipitates the tragedy in the book. Carwin, we are told in *Wieland,* has "indisputably great" intellectual powers (I, 91) and possesses both a vast knowledge and great skill in communicating it to others (I, 95). Although not very much of his background is revealed in the book, we learn from the unfinished work, *Memoirs of Carwin, the Biloquist,* that Carwin acquired many rationalist ideas from his association with Ludloe, an older man who befriended him. Ludloe's faith in the idea of progress and in the perfectibility of man has turned him into a Utopian planner, so that under his tutelage Carwin becomes fired with the belief that a few "enlightened and disinterested" men might establish an ideal state peopled with "a new race" who would eventually "overflow the habitable world."[15]

Thus, in the *Memoirs* fragment, Carwin and Ludloe are both proponents of the radical thought by which the young Brown was so strongly affected, but they are led into serious error by their dependence upon their minds as guides to action. For Carwin is also revealed as a man of great curiosity whose thirst for knowledge had been insatiable but whose education, unguided by any firm moral principle, had been left to his own initiative and understanding. Hence, even before he meets Ludloe, Carwin is capable of fallacious reasoning by which he tries to argue that his ends justify the means he will use to attain them, an error which is only confirmed by his master. He comes to believe, finally, that his duty may sometimes require him to use imposture and that his own best interest may be served by the sacrifice of truth.[16] In short, despite his excellent mind and vast knowledge, the way is opened for Carwin to act as his own passions and desires prompt him, yet to justify those actions to himself by fallacious reasoning. His experience in *Wieland*, therefore, illustrates the errors into which the radical thinker can fall and the evil consequences which may ensue.

Carwin's errors, moreover, become progressively worse as the action of *Wieland* develops. Trapped in the temple by the approach of Wieland, Carwin first uses his power of ventriloquism to extricate himself, believing that his own safety (he is being persecuted by Ludloe)[17] demands his concealment. On the second occasion, thinking that no "inconvenience could possibly have flowed from" the first, he breaks into the conversation between Wieland and Pleyel; and he deceives himself with the thought that he is actually "conferring a benefit on all parties" concerned (I, 219). In each case, he justifies the imposture by convincing himself that it is harmless, or that he is achieving a benevolent end. It soon becomes apparent, however, that, once having used his power, he takes pleasure—as he later tells Clara— in the mystery he creates (I, 220); and his motives, never pure nor untinged with selfishness, increasingly darken as he continues to act. In menacing Clara in her room late at night, he is frankly trying to satisfy the cravings of his abnormal curiosity without regard for the rights of another; and, in trying to frighten her from the summerhouse, he is seeking to maintain a trysting place where he can satisfy his lecherous desires with Judith. Indeed, he even performs a truly monstrous act when he gleefully deludes Pleyel by deliberately blasting Clara's reputation.

Though Carwin may argue the absence of malignant intent in extenuation of his deeds, the perceptive reader sees that he is really a creature almost totally without heart who thinks first of himself and who obviously enjoys the power he can exert over other, less knowing people. More important, he is willing to interfere in the lives of others with his imposture, despite the fact he can never know what chain reaction he may set in motion. Thus, although he maintains to the end that he meditated no harm against the Wielands, by using his power of ventriloquism to escape from the temple, he initiates a series of events that ends only with the deaths of Catherine and the children and with Wieland's suicide. To be sure, when Carwin meets the Wielands some time after he first projects the voices, he tries to explain away the mystery by suggesting the truth, that a physical explanation for them is possible (I, 94-95). But once having opened the mind of Wieland, however unintentionally, to the possibility of his having received direct communication from the Deity, he can never foresee nor control the result which follows. One can never predict the reactions of another, as Carwin learns in his experience with Clara, who does not always act as expected when she hears the mysterious voices.

The career of Carwin, therefore, seems to suggest the dangers that lie in the path of one who attempts to lead his life according to rationalist principles. A great accumulation of knowledge of both men and affairs does not enable one to foresee with any certainty the consequences of his acts on himself or on another —nor can he always be sure that his true motivation is what he thinks it is. Though Carwin resembles Pleyel in his demand for rationalistic explanations of unusual phenomena (I, 94) and is a man of great intellectual ability, he nonetheless falls easy prey to fallacious reasoning and is incapable of resisting the temptation to use his power, even when he knows he should not. A rather cold and heartless villain, he is impelled by selfish motives and is all too willing to meddle egotistically in the affairs of others. Hence, it seems fair to conclude that in the character of Carwin, Brown casts serious doubts on the ability of even exceptional men to overcome their basic human imperfections, or to create a new society where the woes of the present world will be corrected. Indeed, Brown seems to imply that such Utopian planners, left to the guidance of their own understanding, are likely to do more harm than good.

Read in these terms, *Wieland* is clearly a much more important intellectual document than much of the criticism would have us believe. It is certainly not merely the attack on religious fanaticism nor the open exposition of rationalist principles that some of the critics have contended.[18] In fact, one might more reasonably conclude that the absence of proper moral and religious teaching contributes at least as much to the destruction of the Wieland circle as any other factor. To be sure, Clara informs the reader in the very first paragraph of the book that the tale "will exemplify the force of early impressions," and this statement must be taken to mean the baleful influence of the elder

Wieland's mysterious death. But Clara goes on to say that it is also intended to show "the immeasurable evils that flow from an erroneous or imperfect discipline" (I, 25), a concept that can certainly be applied to Carwin's training at the hands of Ludloe and to Clara and Theodore Wieland's education. Clara is quite explicit on the point that their education was influenced by no religious standard, that they were left entirely to "the guidance of [their] own understanding and the casual impressions" of society (I, 42). Such a passage, it seems to me, certainly invites the interpretation that the absence of religious training was a serious fault in their education.[19]

This is not to say, of course, that the book affirms a system of moral or religious value. It does not. A serious weakness in the novel is that possible alternatives to the view which Brown consistently questions are left so disturbingly vague, that no true source for them is even suggested. Thus, in the conclusion, when Clara moralizes on the events of the story, she observes that all the victimized characters, through their errors and frailty, contributed to some extent to their own destruction. And she writes: "If Wieland had framed juster notions of moral duty and of the divine attributes, or if I had been gifted with ordinary equanimity or foresight, the double-tongued deceiver would have been baffled and repelled" (I, 263). Such a conclusion, however, will not do. It does not take into account the sources of error that afflict both Pleyel and Carwin, and it fails to provide any system of value in terms of which the characters could have corrected their errors and acted more wisely than they did. *Wieland* must be considered, therefore, as an intellectually truncated book, the greatest importance of which lies not in the moralized conclusion but in its systematic questioning of some fundamental tenets of the Enlightenment.

VI *Literary Value and Importance*

Indeed, it is this probing quality of *Wieland* that reveals most clearly the book's historical value, for elements in the novel re-echo down the century in a number of different writers. Larzer Ziff has already observed that the theme he perceives in *Wieland* appears again in the works of Hawthorne and Melville (54, 56), but other aspects of the book recur in later writers also. Certainly both James Fenimore Cooper and Herman Melville were concerned with the problem of *Wieland,* for both, in some of their works, raised the question of whether men, through the use of their senses and reason alone, could arrive at a true understanding of the nature of reality. The question informs, among others, Cooper's final novel, *The Ways of the Hour,* which illustrates, through the use of a murder trial, the trouble men have in forming valid opinions on the basis of physical evidence; and it lies at the heart of Melville's "Benito Cereno," in which Amasa Delano fails utterly in arriving at a just interpretation of the reality that presents itself to his senses. Unlike Brown and Melville, of course, Cooper found his affirmative values in conservative Christian belief, but all three are alike in their interest in and esthetic use of the fundamental question.

Other elements too recur in subsequent writers. The intellectual curiosity of Carwin that permits him to experiment on Clara to see if she is really so courageous as she seems (I, 220-21) and that prompts him to invade her room and probe into her journal (I, 224-25) clearly foreshadows the cold and sagacious intellectuality that appears in the heartless villains, like Ethan Brand and Roger Chillingworth, that Hawthorne was later to create. The isolation of the Wielands—their withdrawal from the society of others—and the symbols—farm, house, temple—through which it is expressed remind one somewhat of the thematic use of the concept in Hawthorne's fiction. Indeed, there is even a Jamesian element in *Wieland* when the characters attempt to read each other's motives and emotions, as in the incident in which Clara interprets the look on Pleyel's face to arrive at an awareness of what *his* interpretation of her motives and actions might be (I, 134-35). Such sophistication of technique, of course, is by no means usual with Brown, and he makes no attempt to sustain it. Yet resemblances like these do reveal how much of later American fiction is foreshadowed in this novel.

To insist upon its historical importance, however, is to do the book a disservice, for *Wieland* is well worth reading today for its own intrinsic value. Admittedly, of course, the book contains serious flaws. Like all of Brown's novels, it is structurally quite weak, undoubtedly the result of the haste with which it was written. The Stuart-Conway subplot, introduced early in the book, is soon dropped completely, and Brown brings his tale almost to the end without mentioning it further. He crowds the major part of it into the final chapter, where it appears as a kind of extraneous afterthought and throws the book off balance. Indeed, the whole of the final chapter is rather unfortunate. Supposed to have been written in Europe three years after the main events of the story, it provides the kind of happy ending demanded in popular fiction; and, although it does not detract entirely from the effect of the novel, it is obviously anticlimactic after the preceding chapters in which Clara is finally driven mad by the pressure of events. The ending is a contrived one; and, like most such conclusions, it distorts to a considerable degree both the form and the meaning of the book.

Occasionally, the language of *Wieland* also leaves much to be desired. The latinate words and involved circumlocutions, which several critics have noted,[20] must be considered flaws, especially when they appear in contexts where the effect can only be described as ludicrous. A few extreme examples will illustrate the fault. Thus, in a passage that rather successfully creates a feeling of suspense as Clara listens for whispers in her room late at night, she unfortunately writes: "My habitation was a wooden edifice" (I, 76). Much of the dramatic effect, for the moment, dissolves. Equally serious lapses, moreover, occur elsewhere in the book. On the night of her father's strange death, her uncle hears a loud explosion and dreadful shriek coming from the temple. "The incident was inexplicable," Clara writes, "but he could not fail to perceive the propriety of hastening to the spot" (I, 37). In a similar fashion, her utter fright when murderers seem to be lurking in her closet evokes the expression: "Flight instantly suggested itself as most eligible in circumstances so perilous" (I, 78). Not all of the stylistic faults, of course, are so serious as these, yet one would like to wish them away from a book that has so many really fine qualities to recommend it to the reader.

Errors in structure and style aside, there is much to be said for the skill with which Brown developed the novel. The central part of the story is, in fact, rather well constructed. Between the introduction of the subplot in Chapter IV and the regrettable conclusion, the main plot proceeds at a steady pace, all parts subordinated to the central theme, and moving with a powerful force. Brown's use of his characters to illustrate different temperaments reacting in several ways to a series of odd phenomena was a happy invention. It provided the variety he needed in the development of his theme; yet, at the same time, it enabled him to maintain a central unity in terms of the related meanings expressed or implied through their varied experiences. The action, moreover, moves forward with scarcely a check, each incident developing out of the one that went before with a kind of inexorable force which suggests the lack of control that human beings have over the events they set in motion. The fate of the characters is thus made to appear the logical result of the way they react to external pressures in the kind of world that Brown chooses to posit.

The style of the novel, moreover, despite the serious lapses, fits rather well this mode of development. The short, staccato sentences, reminiscent of parts of *Caleb Williams*,[21] move the tale forward in a kind of breathless fashion, and are, for the most part, perfectly appropriate to the narrator. Thus, in the first chapter of the book, Clara sets the tone for much of what is to follow: "My state is not destitute of tranquillity. The sentiment that dictates my feelings is not hope. Futurity has no power over my thoughts. To all that is to come I am perfectly indifferent. With regard to myself, I have nothing more to fear. Fate has done its worst. Henceforth, I am callous to misfortune" (I, 25).

The movement of the sentences reflects the emotional state of the speaker, and the reader is prepared to accept the paragraph as the proper expression for the obviously distraught person who is telling the story. Brown, of course, does not always maintain this pitch. Indeed, he could not without soon wearying the reader. Hence, when Clara tells of her father's background or describes their pleasant idyllic life before any voices are heard, her sentences lengthen considerably and become calmer in tone. At moments of stress, on the other hand, and most especially when she breaks under the emotional strain of her experience, she approaches the somewhat nervous, but highly effective, tone of the quoted passage.

Most of the book's artistic success, however, derives from Brown's manipulation of the point of view, both in the parts that Clara reports herself and those in which she records the speeches of others. By his use of the first-person technique, Brown is, of course, able to create a great deal of suspense in that the reader has no more information at any time than does the character through whose eyes the story is told. The importance of this device is obvious enough in those episodes in which Clara is faced with danger, and the reader moves along excitedly to find out what will happen. Not all of the episodes, however, are developed at this simple level. The night of the father's death, for example, is largely described from the mother's point of view; and, though the reader is thus removed several steps from the event, the distance rather adds than detracts from the reader's interest. Clara, a child of six at the time, has heard the tale from her uncle, and she repeats the story as he must have told it to her. Thus, Clara reveals what happened through a description of her mother's thoughts and actions, as her father, full of apprehension himself, waits for the stroke of midnight.

The means Brown uses in detailing the incident add greatly to its effect, for he carefully underplays the emotionalism implicit in the scene by describing only the physical manifestations of the characters' emotional states. We perceive the elder Wieland's terror as his wife apprehended it, through his "frequent and anxious glances" at the clock as the hands approach midnight, through the visible shock to his frame as the hour tolls, and through the trembling of his joints that makes it difficult for him to throw on a loose gown. When he goes to the rock, the focus shifts to the mother, and we perceive her emotional state in the same way. Her anxiety drives her from her bed: "She rose, and seated herself at the window. She strained her sight to get a view of the dome, and of the path that led to it." There she sits, anxiously trying to pierce the darkness, when, half an hour later, a light, an explosion, and her husband's shrieks announce the catastrophe (I, 35-37). By describing the scene in this way, Brown maintains both a physical and psychological distance from the event. He makes the remarkable death of the father artistically acceptable and manages to suggest, at the same time, the sense of awe and mystery with which Clara and Wieland naturally look back on the most important event of their childhood.

More important, however, in terms of both structure and meaning is Brown's use of point of view to serve a thematic purpose in the book.[22] Since the story is told through the person of Clara, we see the various events of the novel as they appear to her, and we follow her line of reasoning as she tries to interpret them. But on three occasions, Clara is forced to confront another's account of what has happened, and in each case the shift in point of view brings both Clara and the reader enlightenment. The first occurs when Pleyel accuses her of being Carwin's mistress, an accusation which is all the more startling because she fully perceives for the first time the fantastic errors that one can fall into by simply misinterpreting the true sensations he has received. Both she and the reader know, for example, that she has acted prudently on the night she confronts Carwin in her room, but Pleyel's speech clearly shows how seriously he has misinterpreted each of the actions that she innocently performed. It also reveals, moreover, how plausible is his interpretation of the events—once his mind has been disposed to believe in her infamy.

An even more startling enlightenment comes after Catherine's death, for it does not occur to Clara at first that Wieland has killed her. Instead, when Wieland approaches her after the event, she misreads both his appearance and his actions: first, as indicating that he has not yet learned of his wife's death (I, 171); and, secondly, that he has, and has gone mad with anguish (I, 172-73). When the approach of others makes him turn from her and flee, Clara becomes so distraught that she is hardly aware of what is going on around her. She goes completely mad when she learns of the children's deaths too; and, after her recovery, she arrives at the conclusion—"an unavoidable inference," she calls it (I, 180)—that Carwin is guilty of the crimes. Clara is ripe for her second shock, which comes when she reads Wieland's defense of himself before the court that convicts him—a remarkable document which connotes quite well the madness of his belief that he has acted righteously in destroying his family. Clara is forced to admit, therefore, that Carwin did not actually commit the crimes; but, resisting to the end the belief that Wieland is truly guilty, she insists that Carwin must surely have been the evil influence behind them.

It remains, then, only for Carwin's story to be finally told and the extent of his guilt established for Clara to perceive fully the web of misunderstanding and misinterpretation in which she has been caught. Meeting Carwin at last in her house, she hears him explain the mystery of the voices which all have heard, yet firmly maintain his innocence concerning those which commanded Wieland to kill. At this point Clara hardly knows what to believe. Events come rapidly to a climax, however, with the appearance of Wieland; his attempt on Clara's life, which is thwarted by Carwin; and his ultimate suicide when he learns that he has been the victim of his own illusory sensations. Clara's mind breaks under the strain almost as if it were shattered at perceiving the truth of what has happened, a truth that could not be finally established without the self-revelatory speeches of the other characters. The shifted point of view thus provides the fundamental contrast between events as they are and events as the characters see them that lies at the thematic heart of the novel.

Brown, of course, is by no means so successful as more recent writers have been in integrating all four points of view into a tightly knit whole. There is a certain awkwardness in the way the three speeches are introduced, and they are by no means all equally satisfactory in the handling. In fact, Wieland's address to the court is by far the best. One could wish too that more of Carwin's background had been introduced into his speech—rather than in the *Memoirs* fragment—so that one might gain a fuller insight into his character without going beyond the limits of the novel itself.

To overemphasize these weaknesses, however, would be to miss the point of Brown's remarkable achievement, for *Wieland* is a fascinating book: it is intellectually interesting for its serious questioning of some of the tenets of eighteenth-century thought, and esthetically important for the form in which the theme found its expression. With all of its faults of structure and style, therefore, *Wieland* may well be considered a significant novel in its own right—as well as an important document in the history of American fiction.

CHAPTER 3

Ormond

A S SOON AS Charles Brockden Brown had completed *Wieland*, he set to work at once on another book, *Memoirs of Carwin, the Biloquist*, to recount the early life of Carwin and to describe his education at the hands of Ludloe. Part of the work was written by September 14, 1798, when Dunlap notes he was reading it;[1] but, well before the month was out, Brown had already abandoned it. One can hardly regret the decision. Though the narrative of Carwin's youth is rather well told, especially that part in which he discovers his amazing power and attempts to justify to himself the use of it to attain his personal ends, the book is somewhat less successful in describing the relation between Carwin and Ludloe, the Utopian schemer who takes the boy under his protection and indoctrinates him with fallacious principles. Carwin and Ludloe are too much alike, as Warfel has noted, to provide the dramatic conflict needed in the novel, and the tale bears too close a resemblance "to the pattern of *Caleb Williams* and of the beginning of *Arthur Mervyn*" (114), the opening chapters of which Brown had already published.[2] *Memoirs of Carwin*, therefore, remains an important fragment that is useful in providing information for the interpretation of *Wieland* but is of relatively little value in its own right. The material it covers might better have been integrated into the earlier book.

When Brown laid aside the unfinished *Memoirs of Carwin*, he turned at once to another tale, *Memoirs of Stephen Calvert*, the beginning of which Dunlap reports having read on September 25th.[3] The yellow fever, meanwhile, had disrupted both their lives, and Brown had arrived the day before in Perth Amboy to recuperate from the illness he had contracted in New York. Brown remained there for nearly a month, leaving on October 21st for Burlington, and, eventually, Philadelphia. Back in New

York in mid-November, he was soon at work on yet another book. Brown had bargained with Hocquet Caritat, the publisher of *Wieland,* to complete a new novel, *Ormond,* only part of which had been written. Publication began at once; and, as Brown wrote his brother Armitt in December, 1798, he had to apply himself diligently to the writing "in order to keep pace with the press." So absorbed was he in his work that he was scarcely aware of the passage of time, and he finished each day's task "thoroughly weary" and quite unfit for even writing a letter. Brown had hoped to publish the book before the new year,[4] but the novel did not appear until early in 1799.[5]

I A Feminist Novel

Ormond; or, The Secret Witness, a strongly feminist book, is told in the first person by Sophia Westwyn Courtland, who plays no important role in the action until rather late in the novel. Sophia recounts the life of her friend, Constantia Dudley, an intelligent young lady who exhibits the virtues of constancy and fortitude, who chooses to remain single rather than to contract what she deems are unsuitable marriages, and who makes her way in the world by using her own good sense. Indeed, Constantia Dudley may well be considered the living embodiment of some of the principles Brown had aired in the first two parts of *Alcuin,*[6] and the whole action of the novel well illustrates Brown's attitude toward the rights of women—their need for a sounder education; their right to be treated as free individuals; and their ability, once properly trained, to act in the practical world. An even more radical idea, of course, expressed in the unpublished sections of *Alcuin,* also appears in the book in Ormond's opposition, despite some vacillation on his part, to the institution of marriage. Since such a view is presented, however, as that of an obvious villain, it is clear that Brown did not wish to affirm it as his own.[7]

Other elements as well remind the reader of Brown's previous work. The theme of deceptive appearance, for example, occurs as it did in *Wieland;* it is embodied in *Ormond* in the characters of Thomas Craig and Ormond, both of whom cause great trouble for the Dudley family. The excellent presence and plausible story of Craig—in whose "open and ingenuous aspect," few could fail to place confidence (VI, 97)—allow him to gain the trust of Stephen Dudley, Constantia's father. Craig seems to be all that one could desire, first as an apprentice in Dudley's business and later as a partner, but his true nature is finally revealed by the act of embezzlement that plunges the Dudley family into ruin and triggers the main action of the story. So too does Ormond, the principal villain of the piece, hide his real character behind the mask of apparent frankness and candor to lead Constantia, at the end of the novel, to the very brink of disaster. The truth is almost as hard to discern behind the appearance of things as it was in *Wieland,* and the characters make some serious mistakes in their judgment of men and their motives.

In characterization, too, *Ormond* resembles the books on which Brown had recently been working. The character of Ormond, for example—the proud, intelligent, artful villain—is closely related to both Ludloe and Carwin. All three are—or have been—proponents of contemporary radical thought, and all are willing to use unscrupulous means to achieve their ends. Ormond and Ludloe, moreover, are especially alike in that each is a member of a secret revolutionary organization, modeled upon the subversive Society of the Illuminati,[8] a secret group of "Perfectibilists" which existed briefly in eighteenth-century Europe. Each of the groups to which Ormond and Ludloe individually belong is attempting to remake the world according to Utopian schemes and has for this purpose set up an ideal commonwealth in a secret, remote part of the world. Though Carwin, Ludloe, and Ormond differ in certain specific attributes and talents, all three clearly illustrate the dangerous extremes to which contemporary revolutionary thought can lead the unrestrained thinker. Indeed, Carwin and Ormond, in particular, cause serious trouble to others in giving free rein to their wills.

Even the heroines of *Ormond* and *Wieland* bear a certain—though perhaps only a superficial—resemblance to each other. Each of the girls is an attractive and "enlightened" young lady whose life and happiness are threatened by the duplicity of the villain. Constantia Dudley, a carefully reared girl of sixteen, has, like Clara Wieland, been given an education that raises her above the general intellectual level of her sex. Instead of providing her merely with the genteel feminine accomplishments of music and art, Constantia's father "conducted her to the school of Newton and Hartley, unveiled to her the mathematical properties of light and sound, taught her, as a metaphysician and anatomist, the structure and power of the senses, and discussed with her the principles of progress of human society" (VI, 32). Unlike Clara, Constantia does not live apart from the world. Instead, Brown deliberately thrusts her into the mainstream of life where she meets and survives a series of physical troubles before Ormond even appears on the scene. Her encounter with Ormond, when it finally does occur in the latter half of the book, is also more direct and personal than Clara's had been with Carwin; and Constantia's total experience has, on the whole, a far more positive meaning than Clara's has in *Wieland*.

Constantia Dudley is by far the stronger woman, and the many experiences she goes through are designed to illustrate the constancy and fortitude of her character. After Thomas Craig's embezzlement of her father's funds—a crime made possible by Stephen Dudley's desire for increased wealth and leisure which leads him to entrust the entire business to his young partner—Constantia's mother dies; and the girl is forced to assume the whole burden of the household, when her father first succumbs to drunkenness and then goes blind. Constantia rises to the occasion, but her struggle is a difficult one. The practical knowledge she acquires is painfully learned, for tasks which "to age and experience" would not have been difficult are very arduous to her. She overcomes her initial reluctance to act and executes her duties "with address and despatch. One marking her deportment would have perceived nothing but dignity and courage. He would have regarded these as the fruits of habitual independence and exertion, whereas they were merely the results of clear perceptions and inflexible resolves" (VI, 30).

Brown does not present his heroine as an impossible ideal. Indeed, he goes out of his way to insist upon her defects (VI, 3); he clearly states that she, like the general mass of men, judged "from the most obvious appearances, and was subject, like them, to impulses which disdained the control of her reason" (VI, 41). Though her motives are generally pure, Constantia does not escape the common lot of men, whose decisions are seldom, if ever, "totally uninfluenced by sinister and selfish motives." Indeed, at one point in the novel, her thoughts are swayed by a bias in favor of Ormond, though she herself is completely unaware that they are (VI, 153). Nonetheless, as long as Constantia's problem is purely one of survival in a dangerous—indeed, at times, even hostile—world, her decisions are rationally made and adhered to with fortitude and courage. Thus, when left alone to care for her blind father and a dependent servant girl, Constantia acts decisively. She finds suitable quarters for them to live in; learns how to sew for a living; and, when the yellow fever epidemic reduces her income to practically nothing, manages to survive the plague by buying three bushels of Indian meal and salt—enough to sustain the lives of the three of them for four months (VI, 54-55). Through her foresight, the Dudleys are able to live though the prices of food rise and no work is to be had.

Constantia, moreover, attempts to fulfill her human obligations to the best of her understanding and ability. When her neighbor, Mary Whiston, comes down with the yellow fever, Constantia goes to her; and, at considerable personal danger, she tries to help the girl, whose brother, out of fear for his own life, has deserted her and fled to the country. Despite all that Constantia can do, Mary dies of the disease. Although on the point of collapse, she perseveres to the end and sees that Mary's corpse is properly disposed of. Constantia eventually contracts the disease herself, but no sooner is she up and around again than she visits an old neighbor, Sarah Baxter, whose husband is dying, takes over from the distraught widow, and sets the house aright again. In other human relations, Constantia is equally noble. When, after the plague has subsided, she runs into Thomas Craig, she forgives the wrong he has done her father, lays aside all thoughts of prosecution, and simply asks that he give her some money to relieve her distress. Brown has obviously developed his tale to this point as a kind of modern virtue story,[9] the theme of which seems to be the value of the sort of education that enables a woman to live and act in the practical world.

Such a conclusion is certainly supported by the variations that Brown rings upon the theme, for he introduces two other female characters who go through similar experiences but who stand in strong contrast to Constantia.[10] They are Helena Cleves, Ormond's mistress, whose education has made her fit to be little more than the plaything of men, and Martinette de Beauvais, who turns out to be Ormond's sister, a woman whose freedom and worldly experience have all but unsexed her. Like Constantia Dudley, each has been thrown upon her own resources in the world, for Helena's father dies suddenly and leaves her penniless, and Martinette has been on her own from the time when, as a young girl in Europe, she lost both parents and her foster father disappeared on a trip to the West Indies. Since all three have been placed abruptly in similar circumstances, the way they react to their misfortunes reveals the relative worth of the principles by which they live. Neither Helena Cleves nor Martinette de Beauvais solves her problem so well as does Constantia Dudley. Indeed, both fail miserably.

Like most of her sex, Helena Cleves had been given only a superficial education, one that made her an accomplished musician and a sprightly conversationalist, but did not prepare her "to sustain [the] reverse of fortune in a graceful manner" (VI, 118). She has never been trained to think beyond the day, but has simply eaten and drunk what others have provided. Indeed, as Constantia clearly recognizes, Helena is as "ignorant and helpless as a child, on every topic that relates to the procuring of subsistence," for "her education [had] disabled her from standing alone" (VI, 138). A creature of the senses who can arouse little more than an emotional response in others, Helena falls easy prey to the seductions of Ormond, who, strongly opposed to marriage, takes her as his mistress, despite the fact that she is obviously his intellectual inferior. When the more intelligent Constantia crosses his path, however, he casts his mistress aside; and Helena, devoid of inner resources and unable to bear the shock of this betrayal, can find no solution to her problem but suicide. Thus, in the character of Helena Cleves, one of the best-drawn minor characters in the book, Brown attacks the type of education which makes a woman utterly incapable of withstanding the vicissitudes of life.

At the other extreme is Martinette de Beauvais, a woman whose education has, like Constantia's, enabled her to survive, but who places no limits upon what she will attempt to do. A devotee of revolt and liberty, she has played an active role in the blood bath of the French Revolution and has competed with men in the most masculine of occupations, that of a soldier. If Helena Cleves is wrong in being so dependent upon others, Martinette errs in the other direction by seeking to be completely unrestrained. Constantia recognizes the French woman's error. Although she is at first attracted to Martinette because she believes she sees a likeness to herself in her strange acquaintance, she soon develops an antipathy to her when she learns of the atrocious acts that Martinette can justify to herself in the name of liberty. Constantia listens greedily to all that Martinette has to say, but "not with approbation"; and, although she seeks to learn more of Martinette's past and the deeds that other women performed during the Revolution, she feels dislike replacing her first affection for the melodramatic French woman (VI, 202).

II *The Major Conflict*

Constantia Dudley is thus presented as a kind of golden mean. She is far superior to both of her friends in that she has learned to live independently in the practical world without destroying her moral sense in the process. Her success, however, is not complete. She has one deficiency that Brown does not reveal until she survives her physical trials and faces an intellectual and moral one. Up to this point, Brown seems to say, her education has been sufficient to insure her physical survival; but against the insidious influence of fallacious reasoning and seductive argument, she has not been properly fortified. "She was unguarded," Brown writes, "in a point where, if not her whole yet doubtless her principal security and strongest bulwark would have existed. She was unacquainted with religion. She was unhabituated to conform herself to any standard but that connected with the present life. Matrimonial as well as every other human duty was disconnected in her mind with any awful or divine sanction. She formed her estimate of good and evil on nothing but terrestrial and visible consequences" (VI, 175).

Constantia's weakness derives from a serious fault in her education. Her father, though himself a religious man, had conceived the idea that religious truth could not be taught through "infantile and premature instruction." He strove, therefore, to lead his little daughter's thoughts away from religious subjects with the result that, once she is grown, she comes to view religion "with absolute indifference." It is not that she is opposed to religious belief but that "her modes of study and reflection" had simply unfitted her for discussions of the subject; "her mind was seldom called to meditate" upon it; and, when it did occur, "her perceptions were vague and obscure" (VI, 175-76). Constantia, of course, has enough of a moral sense to be repulsed by Martinette's revelations, and she has, by and large, acted well when confronted by problems of conduct in the everyday world. But, when she is faced with the moral and intellectual challenge of

Ormond, to whom she is attracted but who seeks to make her his mistress, she falls into serious danger.

Her first encounter is innocent enough. Perceiving that Helena Cleves is unhappy as Ormond's mistress, Constantia tries to persuade him to marry the girl and even attempts to change his course of action "by the change of his principles" (VI, 142). In coming to Helena's aid, however, Constantia engages in debate with an adversary she is hardly prepared to meet and who uses unscrupulous means to attain his desires. Constantia, moreover, unwittingly places herself in a vulnerable position; for, as they discuss the question, Ormond perceives her obvious superiority to other women and is soon enamored of her. Indeed, the better Constantia's arguments are, the more convinced he becomes that he can be satisfied with no other woman than her. After the rejection and death of the unfortunate Helena, therefore, he determines to win Constantia by any means. To be sure, "if other terms were rejected, he was willing, for the sake of this good, to accept her as a wife; but this was a choice to be made only when every expedient was exhausted for reconciling her to a compact of a different kind." He pretends, however, to be frank in his treatment of her, challenges her to refute his anti-marriage principles, and even promises her "a candid audience and profound consideration to her arguments" (VI, 174).

What Constantia does not know is that in spite of the apparent candor of her adversary, he is actually a man who has made imposture a matter of principle. Years before, when he had frequently been the victim of the duplicity of others, one incident in particular had had a lasting influence on him. In danger of being misled by the false appearance in a man, Ormond had used his great talent for disguise and imitation to deceive him and thus unmask his designs. Ormond comes to believe, therefore, that he can protect himself from the machinations of others only by such devices—that, although he would like to be open and upright himself, the treachery of mankind compels him to use duplicity.[11] Such are the fallacious reasons he uses to justify his acts, but Brown makes abundantly clear that other motives influence him as well. Like Carwin in *Wieland*, Ormond enjoys the power that his unusual talents give him. It delights him to pry into "the privacy of others, and baffle their profoundest contrivances to hide themselves from his view. It flattered him with the possession of something like omniscience" (VI, 113-14).

The desire for power is indeed a major force in Ormond's motivation. He "aspired to nothing more ardently than to hold the reins of opinion,—to exercise absolute power over the conduct of others, not by constraining their limbs or by exacting obedience to his authority, but in a way of which his subjects should be scarcely conscious. He desired that his guidance should control their steps, but that his agency, when most effectual, should be least suspected" (VI, 173). In his dealings with others, therefore, he pretends to speak openly and frankly, to state impartially the issue to be decided, and to allow the other to make the decision. Yet Ormond's treatment of Helena and Constantia is by no means so rational and honest. He influences the weak Helena in ways that even he was not himself entirely aware of (VI, 120), and he conceals from Constantia the means he intends to use to influence her decision. He hopes to change her opinions concerning marriage "by subtlety and perseverance"; but, should he fail, he is "determined to adopt a system of imposture,—to assume the guise of a convert to her doctrines, and appear as devout as herself in his notions of the sanctity of marriage" (VI, 174-75).[12]

In pursuing his purpose with Constantia, therefore, Ormond is careful never to disclose too much about himself. He does not reveal completely the projects that he has afoot in the world; and, though he seems to take Constantia into his confidence and to answer explicitly all the questions she asks him, his disclosures, although ostensibly candid, always contain an element of obscurity, so that Constantia must always ask again and receive yet another unsatisfactory answer. By this means, he succeeds in guiding her mind in the direction he wants it to take, keeps alive her curiosity without ever fully satisfying it, and leads her on to ever new conjectures and doubts (VI, 173). In a similar fashion, he is careful to conceal from her his fundamental philosophy, for he knows how much it would repel her. Though indifferent to religion herself, she would be likely to consider his views insane. He conceives the universe merely as "a series of events connected by an undesigning and inscrutable necessity, and an assemblage of forms to which no beginning or end can be conceived" (VI, 176). He believes, moreover, that until "the principles of the social machine" are changed, men can accomplish little but evil in the world (VI, 110). Utterly lacking in faith in anything beyond this world, Ormond is violently antireligious. In him, "enthusiasm [had been] added to disbelief, and he not only dissented but abhorred" (VI, 176).

Constantia, of course, is completely incapable of defeating an adversary whom she does not fully understand and who will use any unscrupulous means to subvert her opinions. Indeed, without religious faith, she runs the serious risk of being herself converted to his views. But Constantia is unaware of her peril. She entertains the idea that their differences of opinion concerning marriage might in time be reconciled; and, though she tries to protect herself from self-delusion regarding him, she delights in the lucid letters he sends her while he is away. She is not so foolish, however, as to rely completely on herself, for she discusses the matter with her father and listens to his advice. Strongly opposed to "the political and anti-theological tenets" he has privately discovered Ormond possesses (VI, 177), Stephen Dudley clearly recognizes that, although it might be possible in time to restore Ormond "to the guidance of truth," it will not be done through any power his daughter possesses. Conformity in belief, he knows, "would flow from their marriage, but this conformity was not to be expected from" Ormond (VI, 206). Constantia acknowledges the soundness of her father's reasonings, and agrees to delay her ultimate decision concerning Ormond and to accompany her father to Europe.

These plans are no sooner made, however, than Dudley is murdered, and Constantia would be completely unguarded were she not fortuitously reunited with Sophia Westwyn Courtland, an old friend and the narrator of the tale, who serves as perhaps an even stronger bulwark than Constantia's father. Like most of the women in the story, Sophia has been faced with the problem of making her way in the practical world. Deserted at birth by a profligate mother, she has been reared by the Dudleys from infancy to her seventeenth year; but, when her mother, now gone mad, makes demands on her, Sophia accompanies her to Europe and cares for her until her death. Though she marries a man named Courtland in Europe, Sophia does not forget her old friends but leaves him temporarily and travels to America to search out the Dudleys, from whom she has received no news. When the girls are reunited, Constantia receives a strong ally in her struggle with Ormond, for Sophia, whose name means wisdom,[13] provides the one important element that Constantia lacks: the religious belief that Constantia's education had denied her.

Unlike Ormond, who sees only blind necessity at work in the universe, Sophia believes in "divine superintendence" and knows "that all physical and moral agents are merely instrumental to the purpose that [God] wills" (VI, 217). Thus, Sophia and Ormond directly oppose each other in a struggle to influence Constantia.

Developed thus far, Brown's story seems to be moving toward an inevitable intellectual climax. The reader is disappointed to find that the conflict between Sophia and Ormond never occurs, that the battle for Constantia is won without a struggle. Sophia simply points out to her friend the many serious errors in Ormond's philosophy and immediately convinces her—rather too easily, perhaps, for the artistry of the book—that she "had allowed herself to wander into untried paths, and had hearkened to positions pregnant with destruction and ignominy" (VI, 246). Even more curious is Ormond's withdrawal from the struggle. Ormond had left the city before the murder of Stephen Dudley, so that he is absent when the girls are reunited. When he does return, he makes no further attempt to persuade Constantia to his view. Already aware by some mysterious means of her final decision concerning him,[14] he merely speaks incoherently of obstacles placed in his path and makes strange threats of impending disaster (VI, 247-52). Indeed, he eventually reveals that he has withdrawn from the struggle because he knows he cannot penetrate the defense that Sophia provides (VI, 273). The struggle thus unexpectedly ended, Brown can do little more than conclude his tale with a scene of physical violence.

The events themselves can be quickly recounted. The girls are separated when Constantia, leaving Philadelphia, visits a house she owns in New Jersey[15] while Sophia stays in New York to make the preparations for their journey to Europe, to which Constantia has agreed to accompany her. One evening, just after sunset, Ormond appears at the Jersey house where Constantia, alone, is writing. He reveals that it was he who had driven Thomas Craig to murder her father and that he has just killed Craig himself. He insanely tries to argue that his motive was benevolent, that by the murder of her father he had conferred a benefit on her and would have insured both her happiness and his, had not Sophia appeared to renew Constantia's defenses. Abandoning all hope, therefore, of influencing her to accept him willingly as a lover, he determines to assault her at once. Constantia, fortunately, has a pen knife; and, although she at first resolves to kill herself rather than suffer dishonor, at the final moment she strikes at him in desperation and plunges the knife into his heart. Sophia, full of foreboding over the danger in which she has left her friend, arrives on the scene after the deed is done, takes care of the distraught Constantia, and transports her to England.

III *Artistic Failure*

Such a dénouement, of course, does irreparable harm to the novel; it turns a pair of interesting characters into stock figures of melodramatic fiction and resolves a serious intellectual and moral conflict by extraneous physical means. And most of the damage is done to the characterization of Constantia. In her struggle against the physical troubles that beset the Dudley family, Constantia engages the reader's interest by her forthright, yet feminine, actions; and, even in her first encounters with Ormond, she reveals a staunchness of character that is truly winning. But, with the appearance of Sophia, who dominates her completely, Constantia seems to lose all individuality and to become a mere puppet manipulated by her companion. Her final meeting with Ormond is even more unfortunate; for, as Warfel has observed, Constantia is not allowed to win the victory that by rights should be hers. Had Brown permitted her triumph to come through "a newly won religious faith," Constantia would certainly be a much greater heroine (131). As it is, her physical victory robs her of what should have been an intellectual and moral triumph.

Indeed, for all her strengths and virtues, Constantia Dudley is in many ways a much less memorable character than Clara Wieland, who lays a more powerful hold upon the imagination of the reader. To be sure, Clara is at times rather over-drawn, but her descent into madness is made thoroughly credible, and her intellectual and emotional problems are adequately dramatized. Seen in relation to Clara, Constantia is considerably paler. Her development is weaker, and her intellectual and moral struggle is hardly objectified at all. Besides, Constantia's relationship with Sophia leaves much to be desired. Certain of the critics, indeed, have commented upon its unhealthy aspects.[16] Though Sophia has recently married in Europe, she leaves her husband to search in America for her lost friend. Once she finds her, the two women become as close and secretive as lovers, and Courtland is only briefly mentioned again, even after the two women finally arrive in England. This point should not, however, be insisted upon; for Brown may only have intended to show the closeness of the tie which, considering the fact that the girls were reared together, understandably binds them to one another. Yet at best, the relation is not one to increase the stature of Constantia as the heroine of the novel.

Much the same kind of criticism can be leveled against the characterization of Ormond. A believable villain in the early part of the tale, Ormond is well presented as a man who conceals his deceitful intent behind a pleasant external appearance. To the other characters in the novel, he appears to be an educated and urbane gentleman whose motives are always openly avowed; but, as the action progresses, more of his true character is revealed. We gain an insight into his selfishness and want of compassion, for example, in his treatment of Helena Cleves and in his lack of remorse at her suicide, and we perceive his intellectual duplicity in his discussions with Constantia. We are hardly prepared, however, for his violent actions, insane bombast, and melodramatic posturing at the end of the book, where Brown converts him into a veritable madman. One could argue that a man of Ormond's principles might well descend to this kind of violence[17]—especially when we consider the tales that Sophia relates of his youth (VI, 255-56)—but the shift is not made with enough artistry to be wholly convincing. A character with Wieland's background and temperament may, under sufficient provocation, plausibly become a homicidal maniac without subtle transition; an astute and artful one like Ormond should not be changed so drastically without more adequate preparation.

The deterioration of the characters has a far-reaching effect upon the meaning of the book, for the final struggle in which they engage seriously detracts from the theme that Brown seems to have been developing throughout the tale. The whole movement of the novel has been concerned with the value of Constantia's education in enabling her to survive the physical disasters that she encounters and her inability to win by herself the intellectual and moral battle against the unbelieving Ormond. Indeed, the introduction of the religious theme in the latter half of the book seems to indicate that *Ormond,* like *Wieland,* suggests the need for religious training in the education of the young. Certainly, the absence of religion in Constantia's background reminds one of a similar lack in the education of the Wielands. If, as Brown clearly suggests, his theme concerns the importance of a religious view of the world as the guide to life, one could wish that he had dramatized the conflict more fully and made the religious element more important in the final resolution.

In this respect, the novel is curiously like *Wieland*: both leave the affirmation of value disturbingly vague. To be sure, *Ormond* is considerably more specific, but it fails to say precisely what the religious view should be. Sophia clearly affirms her belief in a divinely directed and purposeful universe, and she looks forward to an afterlife "where woes are at an end and virtue finds recompense" (VI, 231). Her God, however, is most often referred to, in deistic terms, as "the great Author of being and felicity" (VI, 217), or as "a divine and omniscient Observer" (VI, 254), and religion itself is hardly felt as a powerful or dramatic force in the novel. It is asserted as a value rather than lived as a belief. Hence, the reader leaves the novel with a feeling that Brown has not fully expressed his theme, that something more than the general affirmation is needed to make the novel really effective. The book remains interesting for the light it sheds on the development of Brown's thought during his career as a novelist, but it leaves much to be desired as a work of art.

Yet despite the poorly resolved theme and the bungled conclusion, *Ormond*, like *Wieland*, shows signs of Brown's unmistakable talent. Both books are uneven, and their strengths and weaknesses differ. In overall structure, for example, *Ormond* is probably superior to *Wieland* in that it contains no poorly handled subplot left incomplete till the end. In this respect, the action of the book is certainly more unified. Although there are flaws—Brown never wrote a perfectly structured book—the faults lie mainly, as Warfel has suggested, in the imbalance of episodes which are in themselves structurally important and pertinent to the meaning (137).[18] Except for the errors in relative development and emphasis, the action of *Ormond* is, in general, rather well conceived and, up to a point, well executed. From the first disaster that strikes the Dudley family until the introduction of Sophia as a character participating in the action, the main line of development adheres quite well to its central purpose. The subordinate episodes involving Helena Cleves and Martinette de Beauvais are properly related to the whole and add much to the variety of the development and to the theme.

Ormond is probably better, too, in the way Brown handles realistic detail to establish the social environment in which his characters move. Setting is not of much importance in *Wieland,* nor do the characters exist in any recognizable social context. In *Ormond,* the characters live and act in a society that becomes most real and immediate when the plague strikes Philadelphia. Through the use of detail—the rumble of wagon wheels through the city at night; "the shrieks and laments of survivors"; the gaunt and gummy-eyed horse standing quietly before a house while a coffin is brought out—Brown evokes a sense of the stricken town.[19] He manages to render credible, too, the sufferings of the dying and the terror of those who desert their relatives in the city only to die, feared and shunned, in the countryside (VI, 45-50). These scenes are not presented with such circumstantial detail as one might expect to find in later realists, and they represent only a small portion of the book. But they clearly reveal a talent for the realistic in Brown that one might not expect from a reading of *Wieland.*

In point of view and style, on the other hand, *Ormond* is the weaker novel. Less central to the action in *Ormond* than Clara Wieland was in the previous novel, Sophia Courtland hardly functions as a character at all throughout most of the book. Indeed, she serves little more esthetic purpose than would an omniscient narrator, and Brown makes no attempt to exploit the point of view for dramatic—or Gothic—effect as he had in *Wieland.* The point of view has an important effect on the style, for the language of *Ormond* is quieter in tone than that of the earlier book. The reason is not far to seek: the kind of prose that is appropriate to the emotionally distraught Clara would be totally unsuited to the rather staid, proper Sophia. This is not to say that Brown's style has utterly changed. He is surely as fond of the latinate word and involved circumlocution in the second book as he was in the first, and the language of both strikes the reader at times with a rather staccato effect.[20] Because of the change in point of view and style, *Ormond* inevitably lacks the immediacy and suspense of *Wieland.*

Taking the two on balance, one must conclude that *Ormond* is not so successful as *Wieland.* Its virtues are relatively minor.

Realistic detail of the plague-ridden city does not make up for the utter collapse of characterization and thematic development at the end of the book, and a straight—and essentially simple—line of action is really no suitable substitute for the gripping story developed in the major part of the earlier novel. Carwin is, in many ways, a much more interesting villain than Ormond, and Theodore Wieland is a far more credible homicidal maniac. In its broader aspects, too, the earlier book is more satisfying. Although both are intellectually incomplete, *Wieland*, it seems to me, explores its problem more dramatically; and, despite the Gothic melodrama of the mysterious voices, it actually does so in a much more convincing action. The opposition of forces is much too neat in *Ormond* so that the story, in the final analysis, strikes the reader as a rather contrived one. In the light of such evidence, one can only conclude that, although *Ormond* certainly contributes much to our understanding both of Brown's themes and of his mode of expression, the book falls far short of the not inconsiderable artistic success that he had achieved in *Wieland*.

CHAPTER 4

Arthur Mervyn

IN DECEMBER, 1798, before he had finished *Ormond*, Brown wrote his brother Armitt that he had agreed with a Philadelphia publisher to complete *Arthur Mervyn*,[1] the beginning of which he had published the previous summer in the Philadelphia *Weekly Magazine*. Nine chapters had appeared before August 25th, when publication ceased, and Brown in the meantime had gone on to other works. As soon as *Ormond* was written, he turned once again to *Arthur Mervyn* and completed the first part of the novel by February 15, 1799.[2] Published by Hugh Maxwell in Philadelphia within the next few months,[3] part one of *Arthur Mervyn* comes close to being a self-contained unit; and the book can almost be accepted in its own right as a complete, if imperfect, work. It is apparent from Brown's correspondence, however, that he intended to write a second part to the novel, for he consciously left loose threads untied so that he might produce the further adventures of his hero.[4] This second part was published in the summer of 1800[5] by George F. Hopkins in New York.

Although the two parts of *Arthur Mervyn* are rightly considered to be a single novel, critics—with the exception of Berthoff[6]—have generally centered their attention on part one: Mervyn's adventures in Philadelphia before and during the yellow-fever epidemic of 1793. Both Clark and Lewis, for example, give the second part only brief mention;[7] and, though Warfel devotes more space than they to part two, he makes little attempt to discuss it as an important part of a sustained piece of fiction (146-47). The second part of *Arthur Mervyn* is much less effective than the first, but to give so little consideration to the latter half does a serious injustice to the novel. The second part must not be judged merely as an inferior sequel to the first.[8] Rather, for all its obvious weaknesses—and they are many—it forms an indispensable part of a single whole which

CHARLES BROCKDEN BROWN

cannot properly be understood unless both volumes are given the critical attention that is usually accorded to only the first.

I *The First Part*

That part one of *Arthur Mervyn* has been most often praised is perfectly understandable, for the much-admired plague scenes that it contains are, as Lewis observes, clearly superior to other sections of the book (97). Although Brown had used this material for some of the most effective scenes in *Ormond*, those in *Arthur Mervyn* are by far the better. Death and desolation hang over the city like a pall; and, as Mervyn moves through the almost deserted streets, we get a keen sense of the horror of the scene. Some of the episodes are extremely well done—as is the scene, justly praised by Clark as an example of "Brown's power" (180), in which the hearse drivers with business-like efficiency go about their job of collecting bodies from the houses. So inured have they become to human suffering that they are only momentarily concerned that the last victim was not yet dead when they thrust him into his coffin. The circumstantial manner in which the episode is told, and the rather detached attitude that Brown maintains in describing it, remind one—strangely enough—of the technique of Hemingway. Such objectively presented scenes are by no means common in Brown, who tends rather to overplay; but they are, for that reason, the more effective when they do appear.

More typical of Brown's style is the Gothic horror he includes, as, for example, the episode in which Mervyn awakes from a blow on the head only to find some strangers about to place him in a coffin; and, like a character one might expect to meet in Poe, he shudders to think how close he came to premature burial (II, 148-49). Even more terrible is Brown's picture of the hospital, a chamber of horrors where people dread to be taken. The hospital is run by degenerate wretches who are tempted to work by the enormous wages paid them but who ignore the sick and carouse in their private apartments. Their laughter can be heard in the upper rooms, where a dying man cries out for water or begs for help to change his position so that he need not face "the ghastly writhings or deathful *smile* of his neighbour." Occasionally someone enters, and a body is dragged across the floor to a waiting coffin—a fate that lies in store for most of

[66]

the sick who are brought there. Many of those who are stricken, therefore, hide themselves "in garrets, and cellars, and stables" to die in peace rather than face such horrors (II, 173-74).

Brown's picture of plague-ridden Philadelphia is thus detailed and effective, but it is a mistake to assume, with some of the critics, that the realism of the plague scenes is their main value.[9] Realistic though they may be, their primary function in the novel is a symbolic one; they help to define one aspect of a city environment which, as two of the critics have recently shown, serves an important thematic purpose in the novel. To Lewis, for example, the city of Philadelphia is an "impenetrable network of secret and corrupt liaisons" into which the innocent young country boy makes his way (97) only to discover "the prolific reality of evil in every imaginable moral and physical form" (92-93). To Berthoff, the "cruel and poisonous city world" that Mervyn enters is set against "an unpolluted countryside of farms and freemen" and serves as a point of contrast to "the Jeffersonian hinterland" from which the hero originally comes and into which, after his first experience, he escapes. Although Brown, as Berthoff correctly observes, is no doctrinaire agrarian in this book,[10] he clearly intends the commercial city, both before and during the plague, to assume symbolic import as the place of Mervyn's adventures. The scenes of the plague, therefore, reinforce the concept of the corrupt city, one of the most important elements in the first part of the book.

Seen in these terms, *Arthur Mervyn* is a story of initiation,[11] not unlike *Ormond* in that it confronts an innocent character with physical and moral evil and shows the manner in which he comes to grips with it. Yet Arthur Mervyn is not merely another Constantia Dudley. Rather, he is an ambitious young man eager to make his way in the world; and, unlike other Brown heroes, he eventually succeeds.[12] But, although he does finally achieve his goal at the end of the second part, Mervyn's success does not come easy. Indeed, when we first meet him in the opening chapter of the book, he is deathly ill with the yellow fever. He is found by a Doctor Stevens outside a house, his head sunk against the wall, his body held upright only by the cellar door against which he leans. Mervyn, we later learn, has contracted the disease on his second trip to the city and is all but overcome by his experience. Nursed back to health by the doctor, who takes him in, Mervyn eventually recovers. He is recognized, however, by a Mr. Wortley as having been an associate of Thomas Welbeck, whose failure in business almost brought Wortley to ruin and who was last seen in Mervyn's company. Wortley suspects that Welbeck has absconded, and Mervyn is brought under suspicion of wrongdoing when he refuses to reveal anything of Welbeck's whereabouts.

Fortunately for Mervyn, Doctor Stevens does not act on Wortley's suspicions without giving the young man a chance to defend his actions, and much of the story that follows is Mervyn's account of his past. He tells the doctor and his wife that he decided to leave his rural home when his father married a sluttish milkmaid who turned her husband against his son; and, thrown on his own devices, the frail young man, who did not expect to live beyond a few more years,[13] set out alone to make his way in the city. From the very beginning, his experiences are uniformly unfortunate. His first night in town leaves him stripped of both money and possessions; and he soon finds himself, thoroughly gulled, alone in a closet in a strange house where a young man has taken him with the promise of a bed but where he is deserted for a practical joke. Mervyn's position is no laughing matter; were he to be found in the closet by the man and woman who go to sleep in the next room, he would be in serious trouble. Through his own courage and resourcefulness, however, he manages to escape, though he leaves his shoes behind when he does so. Barefoot and destitute, he intends to return to the country at once, but he is distracted from his purpose when he meets Welbeck, who, seeing a use for the boy, takes him into his house as a kind of copyist or scrivener, and starts Mervyn along the path to success.

The story that follows is so complicated that it almost defies summary, yet the complex action must be recounted if the meaning of the book is to be fully understood. Suffice it to say that Welbeck is a villain whose past includes betrayal of a friend's trust, seduction of a married woman, and the consequent destruction of a whole family. Now engaged in some commercial dealings in Philadelphia, Welbeck is obsessed with the idea of maintaining a proper appearance in the world and is more concerned with what people think of him than with what he has done. Like all of Brown's villains, he has a great thirst for knowledge and is familiar with "enlightened" principles (II, 86). Like them, he does not scruple to use others for his own ends. He seduces

Clemenza Lodi, who has fallen into his power, and he frankly informs Mervyn at one point that, by taking him into his service, he intended to do him an injury as well as to confer a benefit (II, 86). Welbeck differs from Carwin, Ludloe, and Ormond, in that he is engaged in no wildly Utopian schemes; he is, when we first meet him, absorbed in what appears to be a normal commercial enterprise. His desire to figure largely in the world and to maintain the kind of appearance that commands respect is at least more recognizably human than the other villains' vaunting ambitions.

For a period of time Welbeck is able to deceive his business associates by the lordly appearance he maintains, but his resources are not nearly so great as he would have people believe. Utterly averse to labor, he tries to keep up his appearance and to replenish his stock of funds by plunging heavily, partly on borrowed money, in a maritime enterprise which seems impossible of failure. The unforeseen event occurs which frustrates all his plans, and Welbeck is brought to ruin. At the same time, Amos Watson, the sea-captain brother of the married woman whom Welbeck had corrupted, appears on the scene and challenges him to a strange duel to which Welbeck agrees only when it seems that Watson will let him live solely for the purpose of destroying his reputation. By an odd chance, the carefully aimed bullet of Watson misses its mark, but Welbeck's random shot kills the captain. At this point, Mervyn, who has served Welbeck unquestioningly for several days, comes upon his master; and, promising never to reveal what Welbeck tells him, he learns the history of his past. Mervyn helps his master bury Watson in the cellar of the house and agrees to row him across the Delaware River. Two hundred yards from shore, however, Welbeck leaps overboard; Mervyn, unable to save him, believes that he has committed suicide.

Only five days have elapsed since Mervyn came to the city; but, as he tells his auditors, he had "gathered more instruction [from them] than from the whole tissue of [his] previous existence" (II, 121). He has been initiated into the corrupt ways of the commercial city, for he learns in serving Welbeck much of the machinations of the business community and has even caught wind of a plot among some of Welbeck's associates to defraud him of a large sum of money. He has seen in Welbeck the contrast between the wealthy, important man he seems to be and the unscrupulous villain that he actually is, and he has also witnessed his act of despair when faced with financial ruin and public exposure. Thus, Mervyn's education in the ways of the world has begun, and to a great extent he is shaken by his experience, because his main desire after Welbeck's apparent suicide is to flee the city. Before the first light of day, he is on his way once more to the country, taking with him from Welbeck's house only a book, written in Italian, that had belonged to Clemenza Lodi's brother.

Part of Mervyn's urge to leave the city results from his fear of what might happen to him if he should remain, part from a desire to find a place where he can exchange his labor for the necessities of life. He turns to the country, then, as his "sole asylum" (II, 119), and he soon falls in with the Hadwins, a Quaker family whose simple life in the rural countryside stands in strong contrast to everything that he has experienced in the city. "The manners of this family," he observes, "quiet, artless, and cordial, the occupations allotted to me, the land by which the dwelling was surrounded, its pure airs, romantic walks, and exhaustless fertility, constituted a powerful contrast to the scenes which I had left behind, and were congenial with every dictate of my understanding and every sentiment that glowed in my heart." Hadwin himself combines "the simplicity of the husbandman and the devotion of the Quaker . . . with humanity and intelligence"; and his daughters, Susan and Eliza, though "strangers to the benefits of an elaborate education," had made good use of the instruction they had received and were totally "unacquainted with calamity and vice through the medium of either observation or books" (II, 124). Indeed, so sharp is the contrast between the virtues of the Hadwins and the venality of Mervyn's associates in Philadelphia that he seems on the point of affirming a belief in the complete superiority of country life.

His rural idyl is soon disturbed by a series of events that leads him back to the city—and, in time, to a considerably different opinion. In perusing Lodi's book, he discovers some twenty thousand dollars in banknotes glued between the pages. Though tempted at first to keep the money, Mervyn correctly reasons that it is not really his but belongs to Clemenza Lodi. He determines to seek out the girl, who, having become pregnant by Welbeck, had been sent from town, Mervyn knows not where. But, before he can embark on his search, yellow fever strikes Philadelphia.

The Hadwin family is seriously distressed at the news, because Susan's fiancé, a man named Wallace,[14] works in the city. When, after a series of letters, Wallace fails to come and nothing further is heard from him, Mervyn decides to go in search of him. Though aware of the danger he incurs, he willingly accepts it in the belief that, because of his constitutional weakness, he will not live long anyway and may at least die helping others. By indirect questioning, he learns from Hadwin the name of the man for whom Wallace works (it turns out to be an associate of Welbeck); and, unbeknown to the Hadwins, Mervyn sets off for the city on a dual mission to locate Wallace, and, if possible, to learn the whereabouts of Clemenza Lodi so that he can give her the money which is rightfully hers.

Mervyn's second experience in Philadelphia continues his initiation into the realities of city life. In noting the effect of the plague on men, he sees both the harshness and kindness of which they are capable. He learns that Wallace was almost destroyed by the self-seeking of his employer, who had delayed his departure from Philadelphia because he feared for his business, and he sees for himself both the callousness of the hearse drivers and the hardheartedness of innkeepers who will admit no one into their hostels. Yet, at the same time, he perceives the benevolence of which other men are capable: Maravegli, who lost his life while trying to help others; Estwick, who saves Mervyn from being encoffined alive; Medlicote, who at one point takes him into his house and offers him food and shelter; and Doctor Stevens, who saves his life when he falls sick with the fever. Thus, Mervyn gains a new insight into the city. He later tells the doctor in the second part of the novel that, although in his first encounter with city life he had "met with nothing but scenes of folly, depravity, and cunning," in his second trip to Philadelphia he not only met a number of honest and admirable men but began to understand the intellectual values nurtured by city life (III, 76-77). The physical evil he encounters is almost overwhelming, but his experience shows him too the more praiseworthy side of the city.

At the moment, Mervyn is only concerned with his immediate problems as he tries to fulfill the purposes that brought him into Philadelphia; and, despite the hardships he faces, he achieves part of his goal. He manages to locate the unfortunate Wallace, who was sent to the hospital against his will by his panic-stricken employer and who unexpectedly survived his stay of several days in that chamber of horrors. Indeed, Mervyn persuades the weakened Wallace to try to leave the city; and, after walking as far as they can, he even procures him transportation to the country in a passing chaise. By this time, Mervyn has himself contracted the disease. Unable to make his way to any place where he might find asylum and fearing that he will be taken to the hospital if he remains in the streets, he decides to hide in Welbeck's house, where he unexpectedly finds himself at the moment of near exhaustion. Here he prepares to wait out the disease or to die unmolested. Much to his surprise, Mervyn once again encounters Welbeck, who, it turns out, was unable to kill himself by drowning and who, suddenly realizing that some unaccounted-for money must be concealed in Lodi's book, has returned to the city to seek it.

Mervyn and Welbeck inevitably come into sharp conflict over the money; for, with his knowledge of Welbeck's character, Mervyn no longer cooperates with, but directly opposes, him. He foresees that Welbeck would only use the money for "the purpose of selfishness and misery" (II, 200), whereas he will return it to Clemenza Lodi, who needs it. The naïve Mervyn, however, is no match for the unscrupulous Welbeck. Though Welbeck's passionate rage is unable to break down his resolve, Mervyn falls prey to the other's shrewdness. Welbeck convinces him that the notes are forged and that Mervyn will only cause trouble if he gives them to Clemenza. The gullible young man believes the story because it is told "with every token of sincerity" (II, 209). When Welbeck turns away for a moment, Mervyn quickly burns them lest they cause trouble to others. Utterly appalled by this act, Welbeck reveals that they were real after all; and, in his rage, he would probably have done Mervyn violence had not people been heard outside who, both of them think, are coming in search of the sick. Welbeck escapes, and Mervyn, though desperately ill, avoids the searchers and attempts to make his way to Medlicote's house. Missing the direction, he sinks to the ground at the spot where Doctor Stevens eventually finds him and takes him in.

The first part of the novel ends at precisely the spot where it began, and, except for the loose threads that Brown consciously left untied, can be read as a completed work. The volume does indeed have a kind of thematic unity, for it details the initiation of a naïf into the ways of a world that almost overwhelms him with its duplicity and physical danger. His experience is valuable, for it illustrates to him something of the contrast between city and country life and prepares him to take his place in the world of men. If we read the book in these terms, Mervyn is seen as a rather conventional hero, a virtuous young man who derives instruction from his experience and resolves, as he does in the final paragraph in the volume, to show his gratitude to those who have befriended him by dedicating his life to worthwhile purposes. Such a conclusion leaves little place for the story to go, except to illustrate the various acts by which the virtuous Mervyn keeps his resolve; and, indeed, something of this sort seems to have been Brown's original purpose.

For, in a letter he wrote to his brother James in February, 1799, Brown makes perfectly clear that he at first intended the second part of the novel to illustrate the virtue of his hero in overcoming the impediments and trials placed in his path. James Brown had objected to the incident, toward the end of part one, in which Mervyn burns the twenty thousand dollars he had found in Lodi's book, but the author defends the episode by arguing that the money must be destroyed because Mervyn "is intended as a hero whose virtue, in order to be productive of benefit to others, and felicity to himself, stands in no need of riches." Indeed, in the plot line Brown describes, Mervyn not only triumphs over adversity but returns to Eliza Hadwin, who, having inherited the farm from her now dead father and sister, marries the hero and thus presents him with "the rewards of virtue."[15] But, although the second part of *Arthur Mervyn* does indeed begin as if it were to follow the plan that Brown sketched in his letter, it eventually comes to such a radically different conclusion that we must defer a final interpretation of either part until both have been duly considered.

II *The Second Part*

The second part of *Arthur Mervyn* begins with a series of adventures that the hero, now recovered from the yellow fever, engages in as he tries to act the part of benefactor to men. At first his acts are perfectly reasonable. Deeply concerned about the fate of both Wallace and the Hadwins, Mervyn leaves the city after he is cured to visit them, only to learn that disaster has struck their rural idyl. Although Wallace had been brought to a country house where he had recovered his strength, he never returned to the Hadwin farm but disappeared. Hadwin, who had gone into the city during the plague to seek Wallace, had himself contracted the disease and died. Susan expires soon after Mervyn arrives at the farm, and the younger daughter, Eliza, to whom Mervyn is attracted, loses her inheritance to a violent and brutal uncle—exemplifying the less attractive side of rural life[16]—who holds a mortgage upon it. Mervyn is thus given ample opportunity to help Eliza by practicing the benevolence he feels he is obligated to show to all, but he soon becomes such an officious busybody as he goes about doing good to others that the reader begins to view him in an increasingly unfavorable light.

Mervyn embarks on an astonishing career of meddling in other people's lives. He finds a country home for Eliza to stay in; and, although he no longer has her money, he goes off in search of Clemenza Lodi, who, he has learned from Doctor Stevens, had been placed by Welbeck in a house of ill-repute. He invades the house to find the girl; meets Mrs. Achsa Fielding, who, unaware of the profession of her companions, has spent the night visiting there; urges her to leave; attempts to help Clemenza; and almost gets shot for his pains. He learns from Clemenza that Welbeck is in debtor's prison; and, much to his erstwhile master's rage, he seeks him out and moralizes upon him, even bringing in Doctor Stevens to try to help the man. From Welbeck, who is on the point of death, they learn of a money belt that Watson wore on his body and that Welbeck has taken from the exhumed corpse. With this belt, which Welbeck surrenders, Mervyn is off to Baltimore to restore what is due the Watson family and some people named Maurice, who have a claim on the money. He performs the task with evident self-satisfaction, but he is somewhat abashed that the Maurices are not so grateful to him as he thinks they should be.

Back in Philadelphia, Mervyn continues his impetuous—almost compulsive—course of action. He succeeds in finding a refuge for Clemenza Lodi and manages to persuade Mrs. Fielding to provide a home for Eliza Hadwin. The more he sees of Mrs. Fielding, the more he becomes enamored of her; and, as the novel approaches its end, it soon becomes apparent that he is going to marry Achsa Fielding, a widow and a mother some six years his senior, who turns out to be a Jewess and whom Mervyn calls his "dear mamma"! The novel ends with the hero rapturously looking forward to his impending marriage.

The conclusion of the tale reveals to the reader, therefore, an Arthur Mervyn considerably different from the lad who walked into Philadelphia one night, only to become the butt of a practical joke. Indeed, he is not the same young man whom Doctor Stevens found outside his house and nursed back to health, and he is certainly not the hero that Brown had intended to develop in his original plans for the second part of the book. To be sure, the later Mervyn is implicit in the first, and he remains to the end something of the naïve boy. In addition, however, there seems to be, as Berthoff recognizes, an unattractive side to Mervyn's character,[17] but this aspect only becomes completely apparent as the second volume progresses.

This is not to say that Mervyn's character is completely inconsistent, or that it changes sharply during the course of the narrative; for, if we look back into the first part of the novel, we find elements in his personality that make his later development both credible and consistent. There is, for example, Mervyn's attitude toward the women he meets. As one would expect of an eighteen-year-old, he becomes enamored of each in turn, but with each he entertains hopes of material success. When he first falls in with Welbeck, Mervyn begins to dream that the older man might adopt him as a son, an idea he seriously considers because "wealth has ever been capriciously distributed" and sometimes results from a "trivial or fallacious" cause (II, 58). In addition, he observes that his appearance, resembling as it does that of her brother, has visibly affected Clemenza Lodi. Since they both live in Welbeck's house, they will inevitably be thrown together. "Time," he thinks, "would lay level impediments and establish familiarity, and this intercourse might foster love and terminate in—*marriage!*" (II, 59). In this connection, Mervyn has not yet looked upon marriage as a step toward material well-being; but both ideas occur to him almost simultaneously at a time when he scarcely knows either Welbeck or Clemenza—indeed, when he has just met them. The dreams, in fact, sound suspiciously like those of an ambitious young man intent on achieving wealth and position in the world.

Such a conclusion is supported by subsequent developments. Once he learns of Welbeck's disaster and of his relations with Clemenza, Mervyn, understandably enough, thinks no more of achieving success through them. Instead, he leaves the city and associates himself with the Hadwins. Again he meets a young woman, Eliza Hadwin, with whom he quickly becomes enamored. Eliza clearly returns his affection; but, when Mervyn begins to think of the future, certain doubts immediately cross his mind. His own labors are light and earn him sufficient subsistence for himself, but they would not suffice if he were married. Besides, though Hadwin's farm supports the family adequately, "divided between his children, [it] would be too scanty for either." It is only when his thoughts reach this point that he remembers another obstacle—that the Hadwins are Quakers, a sect that forbade marriage with one of another belief. Mervyn seriously tells us that he is incapable of hypocrisy, that he would not have attempted to change his opinions or to feign a conversion himself even "if the possession of all that ambition can conceive were added to the transports of union with Eliza Hadwin" (II, 125-26). Mervyn may be perfectly sincere in his statement, but the reader observes that he makes it only after he has decided that marriage with Eliza would offer him no hope for material improvement.

Indeed, as conditions change, so also do Mervyn's opinions; and we are not surprised when, in the second part of the novel, he returns to the Hadwin farm and begins to see things in quite a different light. With Susan and her father both dead, Eliza will apparently inherit the farm; and, since Eliza is now alone in the world, Mervyn does not think that anyone will be hurt if she marries out of her faith. He is also quick to observe that his "own interest could not fail to recommend a scheme by which the precious benefits of competence and independence might be honestly obtained" (III, 75). That Mervyn does not rush into marriage is no proof that he is not self-seeking. He clearly foresees that opportunity might be greater for him in the city, and he wants to defer his decision until he has tasted the fruits of the better side of city life. He soon finds out, moreover, that the farm, which figured so largely in his thoughts, will revert to Eliza's uncle and the girl will be left almost destitute. This information, Mervyn reveals, "necessarily produced a change in my views with regard to my friend" (III, 95); for, although he had previously promised to bring her to the city, he now places her in a house in the country. Such an act is dictated by economic necessity since her means of subsistence are now so small, and he does eventually persuade Mrs. Fielding to take her in. But Mervyn loses interest in Eliza in the ensuing episodes, and one suspects that her poverty is at least partly the reason.

The final outcome of the novel surely confirms the reader's suspicions, for Mervyn soon shifts his affections to Mrs. Achsa Fielding, the woman he ultimately marries.[18] Once again, he believes that there are good and sufficient reasons for his decision. Mrs. Fielding is older, more sophisticated, and better educated than Eliza Hadwin, and she necessarily exerts a powerful charm over the young man. It is small wonder, then, that Mervyn's tenderness for Eliza rapidly fades, but it is also important to note that, some time after he meets her, he learns that Mrs. Fielding possesses a "considerable, and even splendid, fortune" (III, 198). That Mervyn takes this fact into consideration is clear enough in the novel. When he discusses his emotional life with Doctor Stevens, the older man points out as a disadvantage to their union that Achsa Fielding "is a foreigner; independent of control, and rich." Mervyn's reply is revealing: "All which are blessings to herself, and to him for whom her hand is reserved; especially if, like me, he is indigent" (III, 216). It is too much to say, perhaps, that Mervyn deliberately marries money, but the fact that material gain is never far from his mind when he contemplates marriage is surely significant.[19]

It is not only his attitude toward women that reveals the less attractive side of Mervyn's character; his ability to attach himself to an older person who can provide him with the means for material success is nothing short of uncanny. Mervyn comes under the influence of three older men in the story, and with each he manages to advance his career by simply being whatever the other person wants him to be. "A chameleon of convenient virtue," as Berthoff describes him, Mervyn assumes "the form and role that others wish him to assume."[20] This remarkable talent is apparent from the very beginning and is symbolized first by Mervyn's simply donning a suit of clothes. When Welbeck meets Mervyn on the boy's first morning in the city and, seeing a use for him, asks him to come to his house, Mervyn eagerly assents and is duly impressed by the opulence of the residence. Offered a job as a scribe, he immediately accepts, moves into Welbeck's house, and puts on the clothes offered him. His reactions once he dons his clothes—items he describes in loving detail—reveal a great deal about his character.

"Appearances," Mervyn states, "are wonderfully influenced by dress"—a true enough observation, but he seems to confuse the appearance he now presents with reality. Much taken by the figure he pictures himself as cutting—"so well proportioned, so gallant, and so graceful"—he can scarcely believe he is the same person. " 'Twenty minutes ago,' " he says as he looks out the window, " 'I was traversing that path a barefoot beggar; now I am thus.' Again I surveyed myself. 'Surely some insanity has fastened on my understanding. My senses are the sport of dreams. Some magic that disdains the cumbrousness of nature's progress has wrought this change' " (II, 52). So much does Mervyn become what his clothes symbolize that he willingly makes himself the instrument of Welbeck's desires. At his master's request, he agrees to speak of his past with no one but Welbeck, and he even asks for specific instructions on what his master wishes him to conceal. Mervyn is soon rendered uneasy by the promise he has made; but, as he tells his listeners, "these inquietudes . . . were transient" (II, 64). He becomes what Welbeck wishes him to be and seems ready to assume that his new, fancy clothes have wrought a real change in him.

So superficial is the change, however, that it can be put off once again with the clothes. Once he believes that Welbeck is drowned in the Delaware River, he sees the necessity of becoming once more what he was when he first entered the city. The transformation is easily effected. He returns to his chamber in Welbeck's house, disrobes, and resumes his "check shirt, and trowsers, and fustian coat. This change being accomplished, nothing remained," he states, "but that I should strike into the country with the utmost expedition" (II, 120). A simple country man again after his sojourn in the city, Mervyn immediately attaches himself to the first man he meets, Mr. Hadwin, whose benevolence so fills him with "gratitude and joy" that he is willing to become a son to him: "Methought I could embrace him as a father, and entrance into his house appeared like return to a long-lost and much-loved home. My desolate and lonely condition appeared to be changed for paternal regards and the tenderness of friendship" (II, 124). Mervyn is probably sincere as he says these words, for nowhere is there evidence that he is a deliberate sharper. But, at the same time, the reader inevitably wonders at his ability to land on his feet!

Nor is this the last convenient change that Mervyn manages to make; the second part of the novel continues the development that can be discerned in the first. After his second trip to the city, Mervyn again attaches himself to an older man who is willing to befriend him. Doctor Stevens not only nurses the young man back to health after his serious illness, but, after he has heard his story, also entertains the idea of taking him into his family to teach him the science of medicine (III, 4). No sooner is the subject broached to Mervyn than he enthusiastically accepts, his eyes sparkling with pleasure. Indeed, he even manages to make his acceptance sound as if he were conferring a favor on his benefactor; for, he avers, "if my pride should refuse [the offer], I should prove myself less worthy than you think, and give you pain, instead of that pleasure which I am bound to confer" (III, 8). This speech is really brilliant, because it clearly reveals to the reader the degree to which the remarkable Arthur Mervyn succeeds in gaining a personal advantage while professing to his benefactor the most unselfish of motives and the sincerest of intentions.

The reader is hardly surprised, therefore, when Arthur makes his final move and connects himself with Mrs. Fielding, a woman, who, as Berthoff observes, can, like Welbeck—and for that matter, one might add, Hadwin and Stevens—give Mervyn what he wants at little cost to himself.[21] Just as he had done before with the older men, he adjusts himself to her wishes. "As to me, I was wax in her hand," he writes. "Without design and without effort, I was always of that form she wished me to assume" (III, 212). By this time the reader is fully aware that herein lies Mervyn's great talent. His happiness is forever tied up in the wishes of others, and he is always willing to subordinate his apparent will to their desires. In each case, and above all in the last, he manages to profit by the connection. Indeed, with Mrs. Fielding, he acquires a wife and a "dear mamma" at the same time. Moreover, she is rich and he is poor, yet at one point he pursues her with the constant reiteration of the question: "Tell me how I shall serve you. What can I do to make you happier? Poor am I in every thing but zeal, but still I may do something. What—pray tell me, what can I do?" (III, 213). Though part of Mervyn's importunity may derive from his apparent innocence, one implication is certainly clear: he will once again confer a benefit by accepting the gifts of another.

III   *The True Character of Mervyn*

In the light of such evidence, it seems obvious to conclude that there is a side to Mervyn's character that he does not consciously reveal but which is present, at least potentially, from the very beginning of the novel. It is one that even his friends fail to recognize; for Mervyn—like Welbeck before his financial disaster —makes a very attractive appearance and maintains a presence that wins completely many of those who have to deal with him. Doctor Stevens, for example, is strongly attracted to Mervyn from the first moment they meet because of his "simple and ingenuous" aspect, and he informs the reader that he "scarcely ever beheld an object which laid so powerful and sudden a claim to [his] affection and succour" (II, 6-7). The influence that Mervyn acquires over the doctor is further increased by the story he relates. When Mr. Wortley warns Stevens against him, the doctor quite correctly believes that Mervyn should be given a chance to defend himself; but he and his wife are already favorably disposed to hear what Mervyn has to say, and Mrs. Stevens in particular "was prepared . . . to forgive the errors of inexperience and precipitation" (II, 16) before she has even had a chance to learn what they might be.

When Mervyn finishes recounting his experiences—it takes him all of part one to do so—Doctor Stevens immediately accepts his story as the truth, purely on the basis of his own word. It occurs to the doctor, especially on Wortley's prompting, that Mervyn's story could be a tissue of lies. The doctor is a man of experience and knows full well that "a smooth exterior, a show of virtue, and a specious tale, are, a thousand times, exhibited in human intercourse by craft and subtlety." But, although these thoughts do come to his mind and although he makes an attempt to corroborate Mervyn's account, Doctor Stevens never really doubts that Mervyn is telling the truth, even when other people call his character into question. What convinces the doctor is the manner in which Mervyn tells his story and the way he looks when he recounts it. "Had I heard Mervyn's story from another, or read it in a book," the doctor asserts, "I might, perhaps, have found it possible to suspect the truth; but, as long as the impression made by his tones, gestures, and looks, remained in my memory, this suspicion was impossible. . . . He that listens to his words may question their truth, but he that looks upon his countenance when speaking cannot withhold his faith" (III, 13-14).

Other people, however, are not so ready to credit Mervyn's tale solely on the basis of his candid face and glib tongue. Wortley continues to warn his friend against placing confidence in the "smooth features and fluent accents" of his protégé (III, 33); and Mrs. Wentworth, a mature woman who had good reason to suspect that Mervyn was in league with Welbeck, informs him on one occasion that, although she cannot positively disbelieve his story, she will not bestow her faith on his tale without objective evidence. For, she tells him, "there must be other proofs besides an innocent brow and a voluble tongue, to make me give full credit to your pretensions." She is willing to lay aside her suspicions that he has been "an accomplice in some vile plot," but that is all he can expect from her until his "character be established by other means than [his] own assertions" (III, 146). Mervyn does manage to remove the doubts of both Wortley and Mrs. Wentworth. Indeed, Wortley eventually comes to confide in Mervyn's "integrity... as much as he formerly suspected it," and he is won over, Mervyn writes, by his proper behavior (III, 194). Yet the reader remains disturbed when he considers how much of the young man's reputation rests solely upon his own word and his innocent face.

The point of view of the novel helps to create in the reader's mind these doubts of Mervyn's true character, for we never see the events of the story directly. They are always filtered through the consciousness of one or another of the characters. The story is ostensibly told by Doctor Stevens, who introduces Mervyn and provides the frame in terms of which he recounts the incidents of his life. In addition, Mervyn's narrative includes a long digression supposedly spoken by Welbeck, who tells of his previous experience. Indeed, the point of view shifts from character to character until in the second part the device breaks down completely, and Mervyn simply writes the last episodes of the narrative. These stories within stories present some problems of interpretation to the reader. He sometimes finds himself at several removes from the events being described and listening to a narrator—usually Mervyn—whose very purpose is to justify his acts to his friends. Only occasionally does another voice, like Wortley's, enter the dialogue; yet even when the testimony is damaging to the hero's character—and Mervyn's neighbors in the country level some serious charges against him—the strangely talkative young man simply explains them away with a plausible story that is accepted by his listeners.

It is probably true that in most—perhaps all—of these incidents, Mervyn is, as he claims, the victim of deceptive appearance, that things look damaging to his character which are not actually so. But, if appearance is deceptive when others make adverse judgments upon him, how do we know it is not equally deceptive when Stevens and his wife resolve all doubts in his favor? Appearance alone is not to be trusted in either case, yet the doctor gives us little evidence on which to form an opinion of Mervyn's true nature. Other elements in the book illustrate clearly that appearance can be illusory. Welbeck himself had succeeded in deceiving the business community in Philadelphia simply by maintaining an imposing façade, and Mervyn had been duped by Welbeck's apparently sincere representations concerning the supposedly forged twenty thousand dollars that Mervyn destroyed. Thus, appearance has been much too deceptive in a considerable part of the novel—and, indeed, in *Wieland* and *Ormond* as well—for the reader to accept unreservedly the completely favorable judgment that Doctor Stevens makes on Arthur Mervyn's character.

This is not to say that Mervyn is a conscious fraud or that he deliberately lies when he tells the doctor the story of his life. His character is not that simple. Rather, Mervyn apparently thinks that he is being thoroughly honest when he informs us that his motives are pure, that his intentions are good, and that his only desire is to do good to others. Indeed, one can argue that his obvious sincerity is one of the most damaging elements in his character in that it seems to suggest a kind of self-deception on Mervyn's part which enables him to get what he wants materially out of life without cost either physically or emotionally to himself and which allows him at the same time to preen himself on his own benevolence. He succeeds, but he apparently truly believes that he has done only good in the process. Certainly the contrast between his professions and his acts, between the ends he supposedly seeks and the ones he attains, suggests an interpretation of this sort. One may perhaps agree with Berthoff that we should not make too much of Brown as a conscious ironist in his treatment of Arthur Mervyn,[22] yet Berthoff's suggestion itself is provocative—for the development of the novel clearly reveals an irony that the modern reader simply cannot ignore.

This suggests that Charles Brockden Brown wrote better in *Arthur Mervyn* than he had intended, since the view we get of the hero by the end of the second part is certainly more complex and more interesting than the one Brown originally planned. His method of composition and the length of time over which the novel appeared[23] undoubtedly account for the change. The plots of Brown's novels, as has been noted, developed as he wrote them, with incident suggesting incident as the work progressed. One suspects that the character of Arthur Mervyn grew and developed under his hand as the second part was written. The result is pure gain for the reader and for Brown's reputation as a novelist: the picture of the hero we finally see in the latter part of the book is a triumph of characterization. Much of the naïveté of the original character remains, but other elements in his make-up have also been developed to turn him into a much more realistic and believable—though certainly a less admirable— character than he had first appeared to be at the beginning of the novel.

In *Arthur Mervyn*, Charles Brockden Brown created a story that is most notable, not for the justly praised realism of the plague episodes, but for the remarkable portrayal of the hero's character. Arthur Mervyn stands out as the most complex portrait that Brown had drawn. Beside him, such characters as Wieland and Ormond, well presented though they sometimes are, seem overly simple in development, and even Clara Wieland is much his inferior. All three at times tend to be overdrawn and lapse into the melodramatic. Yet, if Mervyn escapes the excesses that sometimes mar these characters, he also develops beyond the character of simple virtue that Brown had created in Constantia Dudley. Indeed, of all the characters we have discussed so far, only Carwin compares at all with Mervyn in his ability to justify his acts by rationalized motives, and even he lacks the subtlety and ambiguity that make the revelation of Mervyn's character so absorbing to the reader. It is easier to recognize the selfish motivation that lies behind Carwin's deeds, whereas Mervyn's motives, disguised even to himself perhaps, are always presented as pure and benevolent.

In other elements, too, *Arthur Mervyn* marks a departure from Brown's other work. In its emphasis upon the rise of its hero to a successful position in life and in the picture of both urban and rural society revealed in the process, the book comes closer in subject matter and technique to what might be called a modern novel than do his previous books.[24] In theme there are new developments too. Although some of the concepts—most notably that of deceptive appearance—are present here as they were in *Wieland* and *Ormond*, new ones are developed which show Brown's deep, continuing interest in moral and intellectual questions. Surely the emphasis that Arthur Mervyn places on his benevolent intent, especially throughout the second part of the novel, and the ends he manages to attain while professing benevolist principles suggest to the reader that Brown is raising serious doubts about the validity of such concepts as the sole guides to action. The effect of Mervyn's deeds is to call into question the principles he so glibly asserts, so that the book as a whole may legitimately be read as a strong counterstatement to the benevolist principles by which Mervyn claims to live.[25]

Yet, despite the well-drawn character of the hero and the intellectual interest that the novel generates, *Arthur Mervyn* is not a completely satisfactory book. It bears the signs of haste that mar all of Brown's novels, and it fails in a number of important qualities. The plot, especially in part two, is a maze of incidents; and the reader must work his way through a confusing series of events, not all of which are properly proportioned to the book's primary end. Thus, the novel as a whole lacks the clarity of structure that is apparent in at least the major parts of *Wieland* and *Ormond*. Much of the trouble derives from the point of view, for Brown did not handle successfully the stories within stories that make up so much of the book. In the hands of a Faulkner, the device can be an effective one,[26] but Brown was unable to carry it through to a successful conclusion. Except for the long digression by Welbeck, the technique works well enough in part one, which has a roundness and completeness in its structure that is rather satisfying. In the second part, the first-person technique fails utterly to carry the story along, and the book becomes diffuse and confusing in its development. This method of telling his story was much too ambitious for Brown; he wrote too fast and revised too little to make it work.

Arthur Mervyn remains yet another of Brown's interesting and significant failures: with all its obvious faults in structure and presentation, it is a fascinating book. The setting of the novel has, at times, a reality seldom apparent in Brown's other books, and much of it serves a thematic purpose, at least in the first part of the novel. The scenes of the yellow fever in Philadelphia are drawn in convincing detail and serve as a meaningful contrast both to the rural countryside and to the more pleasant aspects of city life as represented by Doctor Stevens and the other virtuous men whom Mervyn learns of or encounters. All of these elements, however, are of but secondary importance to the character of Arthur Mervyn himself, whose climb to success is really beautifully done. The recurring pattern of action revealed as Arthur moves between city and country, his attachment to women who seem able to provide him with material possessions, his relation to older men who can further his career, his willingness to be whatever the person who helps him wants him to become—all reveal the essential contradiction between his professed motives and his actual deeds which fixes his character unmistakably in the reader's mind. For all its faults, *Arthur Mervyn* remains a book well worth reading, if only because of the fine portrayal of Brown's most complex character.

CHAPTER 5

Edgar Huntly

IN TREATING the two parts of *Arthur Mervyn* as a single novel, we have been forced to disregard the chronological order of Brown's works, for the second part of that book did not appear until over a year after the first. In this interval Brown had engaged in a number of important activities. He had launched his first periodical, *The Monthly Magazine and American Review,* in the spring of 1799; and he had published his fourth major novel, *Edgar Huntly; or, Memoirs of a Sleep-Walker.* A selection from this work appeared in the first issue of Brown's magazine in April, 1799, and the book seems to have been ready for the press by July of that year. Published by Hugh Maxwell in Philadelphia, who had brought out the first part of *Arthur Mervyn,* the copies were on sale by late summer.[1] *Edgar Huntly,* therefore, stands midway between the two parts of *Arthur Mervyn,* a book which, in certain respects, it resembles; it too is, as Berthoff and Fiedler have observed, an initiation story[2] which details the experience of a young man who learns much about himself and the world as a result of his adventures.

I *A Literary Innovation*

Having said this much, one must hasten to add that *Edgar Huntly* is not another *Arthur Mervyn;* it is, in some important ways, a very different book. Most significant, perhaps, is the fact that *Edgar Huntly* looks in two directions at once. It not only marks a return to the kind of psychological novel Brown had written in *Wieland,* but also represents in the material it treats an important innovation both in Brown's career and in American literature itself. Up to this time, most of Brown's best writing had been concerned with man in a civilized environment—a semi-rural one in *Wieland* and the city of Philadelphia in *Ormond* and in much of *Arthur Mervyn*. In *Edgar Huntly*, however, Brown turns away from the civilized society he had previously treated to set the major events of his novel on the upper reaches of the Delaware River not far from the actual wilderness. Part of the action does take place in a relatively settled rural area, but the best episodes by far occur in the untouched wilderness and deal with a subject matter that, in the hands of later writers, was to become a staple of one type of American fiction—frontier war with the Indians.

That Brown was the true innovator in using this material has been pointed out by his biographers,[3] and his probable influence on James Fenimore Cooper, who comments unfavorably on a scene in *Edgar Huntly* in his first Preface to *The Spy*, has occasionally been suggested.[4] Brown's treatment of the Indians is much different from that of Cooper. With the exception of Queen Mab, an old woman who is shown to have some individual qualities, Brown's Indians are stock enemy figures who have no romantic attributes. Ruthless in warfare and cruel to their captives, they are dogged, determined foes who attack the settlements to kill and burn in cold blood.[5] The settlers, too, it must be added, are equally fierce in their resistance. They yield no quarter in defense of their homes; and Huntly himself, though much averse to shedding blood, is forced to kill five Indians in the course of his adventure, finishing off the last, whom he had only wounded, with a bayonet. Such scenes of frontier violence are new to Brown's fiction and illustrate his attempt to turn the realities of American frontier life to literary advantage.[6]

More important, in view of the line of development that American literature was soon to follow, is Brown's use of untouched nature as a significant element in the novel. The most sharply drawn scenes in his earlier books had always been the urban ones; and the natural setting, when it was mentioned at all, served almost as a static—and not very interesting or important—backdrop to the action. In *Edgar Huntly* the tangled wilderness of the Norwalk district, which plays so important a role in the novel, is described in some detail, and it is precisely the wildly romantic aspect of the area that is most stressed. Huntly is devoted, he tells us, "to the spirit that breathes its inspiration in the gloom of forests and on the verge of streams"; and he loves "to immerse [himself] in shades and dells, and hold converse with the solemnities and secrecies of nature in the rude retreats of

Norwalk" (IV, 90). Such an attitude had as yet found no expression in Brown's major fiction.[7] It marks a complete departure from the concepts expressed in his previous books, and it points ahead to the use of the wilderness scene that we later find in the works of James Fenimore Cooper.

To stress these forward looking aspects of *Edgar Huntly* is to court the serious danger of distorting the meaning of the book, for the temptation is strong to see these elements as having an importance in themselves alone—one independent of the thematic function that they were designed to serve. Thus, although a number of critics have commented upon the historical importance of the frontier episodes and have praised Brown highly for his use of the materials,[8] little attempt has actually been made to show their function in the developing theme of the novel. One critic at least has gone so far as to state that the scenes of frontier violence bear no relation to the abnormal psychological state of the hero.[9] The relation is not at first apparent, for the sheer physical excitement of the episodes obscures, perhaps, their thematic function. Yet a case can certainly be made for these scenes as representing in themselves a kind of projection of Huntly's mental condition. Indeed, the tangled confusion of the untouched wilderness may well be read as an index to the hero's mind—just as the forest in some of Hawthorne's works can be seen as a symbol of the moral state of his characters.

Such a conclusion is certainly suggested in the early pages of the book, in which a relationship is established between the hero's mind and the external scene. As the story begins, Huntly, alone and at nightfall, is walking home toward Solesbury from a visit to his sweetheart, Mary Waldegrave, who lives in another town and whose brother, Huntly's close friend, has recently been murdered. That Huntly must travel at night is of little concern to him: as he tells us, "a nocturnal journey in districts so romantic and wild . . . was more congenial to my temper than a noonday ramble" (IV, 6); and this opinion is clearly evidenced in subsequent events. As night falls, Huntly's "sensations [sink] into melancholy"; and, approaching the general area where the murder took place, he recalls the "insanity of vengeance and grief" (IV, 7) which he had first experienced at his friend's death, but from which he since recovered. Nevertheless, his mind reverts to feelings of bitterness and revenge; and, as a result, he is driven compulsively to the site of Waldegrave's murder—a huge elm tree "on the verge of Norwalk"—even though his path is along a different route (IV, 9). Huntly has thus turned out of his proper way to seek this isolated spot. In doing so, he triggers a series of events that eventually leads to his thrilling frontier adventures at the end of the book.

II *Psychological Development*

At this point in the novel, Huntly, who narrates the tale himself in a long letter to Mary, is aware of his mental aberration and is able to compare his first insane reactions at Waldegrave's death with his later recovery and his relapse. The reader is amply warned that in *Edgar Huntly* he faces a problem of interpretation more difficult than that presented by *Wieland* or by *Arthur Mervyn*. The tale is told by a narrator in imminent danger of losing control over his mind and emotions, and the reader is forced to look behind the episodes described to learn the real truth of the events. Once aware that Huntly is drawn to the tree by a strange compulsion which impels him to search the spot once again—he has already done it "a hundred times" (IV, 8)— for clues of the murderer, the reader should be on his guard to question the professed motives and purposes of the narrator. If Huntly slips once again into a mentally disturbed state, he will not be aware of it himself, and the reader will have to perceive it through words and actions which to Huntly seem perfectly reasonable.

Edgar Huntly does indeed soon lapse into this unfortunate condition. As he approaches the elm tree where Waldegrave died, he sees a strange figure busily digging the earth beneath it and filling the air with sobs of grief. Huntly is at first deeply moved by the scene, but he soon reaches the conclusion—natural enough, perhaps, under the circumstances—that the stranger has had some connection with Waldegrave's death and that he need only make this man the subject of his scrutiny to solve his friend's murder. This thought gives Huntly evident satisfaction because "it seemed as if the maze was no longer inscrutable. It would be quickly discovered who were the agents and instigators" of Waldegrave's murder (IV, 15). That Huntly has indeed been involved in an intellectual maze is obvious enough from the opening pages of the novel, but that his suspicions of the mysterious stranger and his desire to make him the object of his study are likely to lead him out of it must be questioned. He seems rather to be giving in to the strange compulsions that have heretofore moved him, and it is much more likely that his mental troubles will only be intensified by his actions.

The ensuing episodes clearly support this conclusion. Huntly eventually recognizes the stranger as Clithero Edny, a servant at Inglefield's, a nearby farm, but at this moment he merely perceives that the as yet unidentified man is walking in his sleep. Huntly observes that such a phenomenon denotes "a mind sorely wounded" and concludes that the man has perpetrated "some nefarious deed," most likely the murder of Waldegrave (IV, 13). Yet if the inability to sleep soundly indicates a deeply troubled mind, Huntly himself is in emotional difficulty, for he ponders so much on these matters that his own "slumbers were imperfect" (IV, 16). And the following night he returns to the elm tree to see if he can learn the truth from Clithero. He waits for his arrival for all of an hour when he suddenly perceives him there. This night, however, Clithero does not dig but muses for a while and then bursts forth "into sighs and lamentations." When Clithero rises to go, Huntly determines "to tread, as closely as possible, in his footsteps"; and he pursues him first "along an obscure path" and then "through a most perplexing undergrowth of bushes and briers" (IV, 17-18). The action of neither man is normal, and one is certainly justified in reading a symbolic meaning into such strange behavior.

Seen in this light, the journey of Huntly into the region of Norwalk bespeaks the developing madness in a man who has left his normal path to satisfy his irrational compulsions. Clithero leads the way through a difficult labyrinth, hurries along the verge of a precipice, descends into a valley, and eventually buries himself in a cave. Later one learns that the cavern has often served Clithero as a place to brood over his sorrows (IV, 85) so that it comes to be the symbol of a mind possessed; but, even without this clue to its interpretation, one could still recognize the cave as the external expression of an obsessive mental state and the journey into the wilderness as movement through an intellectual labyrinth that can only terminate in such a place.[10] Huntly's mad pursuit of Clithero thus provides a clear indication of his unbalanced mind. Indeed, he realizes himself that his mad career had taken him through "a maze, oblique, circuitous," in which "all dangers were overlooked, and all difficulties defied.

I plunged into obscurities, and clambered over obstacles, from which, in a different state of mind, and with a different object of pursuit, I should have recoiled with invincible timidity" (IV, 23). Nonetheless, he continues his mad career. Driven, like other of Brown's characters, by an obsessive desire to know, he is determined to learn the reasons for Clithero's strange behavior.

The truth turns out to be something quite different from what he had expected. Convinced that Clithero is the murderer of Waldegrave, Huntly confronts him with his suspicions; Huntly is certain that he has drawn just inferences from the events he has observed and is filled with benevolent feelings that he can lead the unfortunate man back to virtue. In this state of mind, Huntly resembles both the characters in *Wieland*, who believe they can arrive at truth through the interpretation of sensory evidence, and the benevolent-minded Arthur Mervyn, who is always sure his motives are good even when he is pursuing selfish ends. Like all of these other characters, Huntly is shown to be in error in the inference he has made and in his belief that benevolent feelings are sufficient to lead him to proper ends. Indeed, Clithero informs him of his errors at once. "The inferences which you have drawn, with regard to my designs and my conduct," Clithero tells him, "are a tissue of destructive errors. You, like others, are blind to the most momentous consequences of your actions." Although Huntly had intended to do him good, his "misguided zeal and random efforts," Clithero argues, will do him harm instead (IV, 34-35).

To illustrate his contention, Clithero, in a long digression, relates the story of his life. The son of Irish peasants, he had attracted the attention of a widow, Mrs. Lorimer, who took him into her household, educated him, and made him the companion of her son. Although he and the son soon part company because of Clithero's somewhat censorious criticism of his behavior, he is retained in Mrs. Lorimer's family in a position of trust and becomes engaged to Clarice, his patroness's niece. This girl is the daughter of Arthur Wiatte, Mrs. Lorimer's twin brother, who, although still retaining his sister's deep affection, is described as so utterly depraved as to be a remorseless villain. He has hurt his sister deeply by managing to drive away her lover, Sarsefield, and by urging their parents to marry her to another. After the parents' deaths, he wastes the patrimony and eventually becomes a highwayman. When he is sentenced to be transported for his crimes, his sister refuses to intercede on his behalf, for she knows that his vice is incurable and that this punishment is the most lenient he can expect. Wiatte is thought to have died in a mutiny aboard the ship in which he sailed, but Mrs. Lorimer, under the delusion that their lives must end together, continues to believe that he is still alive. Meanwhile, Sarsefield, who has spent many years in India and America, returns to renew his acquaintance with the family.

At this point, Wiatte once again appears upon the scene and precipitates Clithero's tragedy. Returning one evening from delivering a sum of money to a banker, Clithero is walking through a dark lane when a man steps to his side, fires a shot that grazes his forehead, and draws a knife to kill him. By a kind of reflex action, Clithero, on seeing the glint of the knife, draws a pistol and fires, mortally wounding his assailant. Clithero, of course, does not know who his attacker is, and Brown has arranged the incident in such a way that no guilt can be assigned to Clithero in preserving his own life. Some of the people who rush to the scene know him, the case is easily explained, and Clithero is allowed to go on his way unchallenged. When the assailant is carried out of the lane and into the light, Clithero immediately recognizes him as Mrs. Lorimer's brother. This recognition sets Clithero's mind off on a line of thought that leads to appalling consequences. Understandably upset by what has happened, Clithero loses his power of clear thought and reasonable action. In a kind of mental stupor, he wanders back unconsciously almost to the banker's door; but, more important, strange thoughts arise in his mind to torment him.

He begins to think how much the knowledge of Wiatte's death will afflict Mrs. Lorimer, who not only wishes her brother no harm but also believes that she must die when he does. Clithero madly reproaches himself for what he has done and actually thinks himself an ingrate because he has purchased his life at the price of her sorrow. "My fancy began to be infected with the errors of my understanding," he states. "The mood into which my mind was plunged was incapable of any propitious intermission. All within me was tempestuous and dark" (IV, 73). He begins to think that perhaps Mrs. Lorimer is already dead, and he rushes to her room to test the truth of his fears. But even the sound of her steady breathing fails to calm him, for he begins to fear what she will suffer when she wakes to learn the truth; and he actually resolves to kill her himself to protect her from that knowledge. At the point of striking her with a dagger, however, he hears a shriek behind him; Mrs. Lorimer herself diverts the blade; and Clithero learns that he has almost stabbed Clarice, who is in her aunt's bed. Mrs. Lorimer faints away on hearing of her brother's death; and, convinced that she is dead, Clithero flees the house, eventually to make his way to America.

Having disburdened himself of his story, Clithero disappears into the wilderness and leaves Huntly alone to muse on his tale. Huntly is fascinated by the story, both because it involves Sarsefield—who, one learns, had become his friend and mentor while he was in America—and because of the nature of the tale itself. But, instead of convincing him that his inferences are erroneous and his benevolent feelings misdirected, as Clithero had evidently expected, it seems rather to confirm him in error. Though he realizes his suspicions were wrong, he interprets Clithero's conduct as "an act of momentary insanity" originating in a "spirit of mistaken benevolence" and considers it "the fruit of an ardent and grateful spirit" (IV, 86-87). Huntly argues that Clithero is really blameless, not only in his killing of Wiatte but also in his attempted murder of Mrs. Lorimer; for, in his opinion, Clithero "desired to confer on her the highest and the only benefit of which he believed her capable. He sought to rescue her from tormenting regrets and lingering agonies" (IV, 106). His defense of Clithero is not simply that the servant was insane at the time of his act but that his intent was benevolent! The reader is thus clearly warned that Huntly's own benevolent purposes may be equally mad and lead to similarly disastrous results.

III *Descent into Madness*

Huntly does not realize that his acts are anything but rational. As obsessed now with the idea that he must help the unfortunate Clithero as he had previously been with seeking Waldegrave's murderer, Huntly determines to follow Clithero into the wilderness, though he realizes it is unlikely that he will be able to locate him there. Thus, once again following Clithero's lead, Huntly plunges into the labyrinth that Clithero has repeatedly threaded and penetrates the cave where he has brooded over the past. Aware as the reader is of Clithero's madness, he can only in-

terpret Huntly's pursuit of him into Norwalk as an objective projection of Huntly's own descent on the same path to insanity.

Indeed, Huntly is relentless in his pursuit. Making his way
through the cavern to an isolated peak in the wilderness, he
actually finds Clithero sitting on the far side of a deep chasm
in a position that seems totally inaccessible. Determined that his
benevolent intention to restore Clithero to sanity shall not be
frustrated—feelings that may perhaps derive from his own guilt
in driving Clithero into the wilderness by prying into his past—
Huntly makes repeated trips between the farm and Norwalk,
fells a tree across the chasm so that he may approach the spot
where he saw Clithero, and even leaves food where he thinks
he will find it.

Like Arthur Mervyn, Edgar Huntly engages in strangely compulsive actions which he justifies to himself as purely benevolent.
As time goes on, the reader increasingly recognizes how far from
normality his actions really are. Impelled by his strong curiosity,
Huntly pries relentlessly into Clithero's past. He examines the
locked box that Clithero had left at Inglefield's farm and works
on it until he releases a hidden spring that opens it. Though he
finds nothing of interest inside, he learns to his consternation
that he cannot close it again—a symbol, perhaps, of his inability
to foresee or control the consequences of his acts. He even digs
beneath the elm tree where he had first seen Clithero walking
in his sleep and turns up another locked box buried beneath the
turf. On his return to Inglefield's that same night, Huntly is
surprised to learn that Clithero has come back, destroyed the
box whose secrecy Huntly had violated, and disappeared again.
But even this knowledge does not deter Huntly from smashing
the box that he has just dug up, nor from reading the manuscript,
written by Mrs. Lorimer and defending her actions in regard to
her brother, that Clithero had concealed in it.

So far down the path of irrational action has Huntly gone that
he even begins to act like Clithero himself.[11] For just as the
unfortunate servant has preserved Mrs. Lorimer's manuscript, so
also has Huntly kept a package of letters written by his murdered
friend. Both take extraordinary steps to preserve their papers,
and both unconsciously hide them while walking in their sleep.
Indeed, both have feelings of guilt regarding the authors of the
manuscripts. Clithero, of course, thinks he has caused his patroness's death; Huntly, that he has failed to fulfill his friend's wishes.

Huntly's belief is revealed in a strange dream that he has one night. "During my sleep," he writes, "the image of Waldegrave flitted before me. Methought the sentiment that impelled him to visit me was not affection or complacency, but inquietude and anger. Some service or duty remained to be performed by me, which I had culpably neglected: to inspirit my zeal, to awaken my remembrance, and incite me to the performance of this duty, did this glimmering messenger, this half-indignant apparition, come" (IV, 124). The dream is powerful enough to disturb his sleep, because he awakes long before his accustomed hour and thinks immediately of his manuscripts.

These letters are the cause of his guilty feelings, for most of them were written by Waldegrave during a period of irreligious thought when he attempted to persuade Huntly to accept his new intellectual views. Because Waldegrave later changed his mind and, in a series of conversations, tried to influence Huntly to return to religious belief, Waldegrave had pleaded with his friend to destroy the letters lest they lead someone astray. Huntly still remains somewhat influenced by the arguments that the letters contain; and, unwilling to part with any remembrance of his friend's active mind, he has failed to comply with his request. Worse, he has even promised Mary, albeit reluctantly, to send her copies of her brother's letters; and he now begins to fear that, by fulfilling his promise to her, he might make the dead Waldegrave the unwilling cause of his sister's apostasy. On awaking from his strange dream, Huntly thinks these matters over and finally decides to send her only the sections which might be considered safe for her to read. When he goes to the cabinet to get the letters, however, he is aghast to find them missing.

Their disappearance is completely inexplicable to him: no one but Mary knows of their existence, and he has kept them locked in a cabinet as cunningly contrived as Clithero's box. The key to the cabinet is always kept in a locked box, and the drawer within the cabinet, where the manuscripts are deposited, can only be opened, like Clithero's box, by a secret spring. Utterly at a loss to explain what has happened, Huntly is struggling with his problem when his uncle knocks at the door to ask why he has been acting so strangely during the night; he thinks he has heard him pacing back and forth on the top story of the house. It does not occur to either of them that Huntly has begun to sleepwalk, and it is not until the end of the novel that the full truth is revealed. Huntly and Clithero have acted in precisely the same manner. While still asleep, Clithero had removed his manuscript from his trick box and buried it under the elm tree. In a similar fashion, impelled by his feelings of guilt at not having obeyed his friend's injunction, Huntly arises after his dream, performs while still asleep the complicated process of opening his cabinet, and conceals his manuscripts "between the rafters and shingles" of his uncle's roof (IV, 249, 267).

Thus driven by fears and compulsions into acts that parallel those of the mad Clithero, Huntly is rapidly losing complete control of his actions and needs only one additional shock to push him completely over the line into madness. That shock comes almost immediately. Although anxious to seek out Clithero in the wilderness once again, Huntly decides to remain at home the following night to recoup his strength. While sitting alone in the parlor, he is visited by a stranger who brings distressing news. The visitor, named Weymouth, had been a friend of Walde-grave;[12] and, while on a speculative voyage to Europe to engage in trade, he had consigned a large sum of money to Waldegrave for safekeeping before his return home. Shipwrecked off the coast of Portugal on his homeward voyage, Weymouth had been long delayed only to learn on his arrival that Waldegrave was dead. Unable to locate any relatives, he is directed to Edgar Huntly as the man who might know of Waldegrave's affairs. Huntly had indeed found a large sum of money in Waldegrave's estate, a sum that neither he nor Mary could explain since Walde-grave's occupation, the teaching of Negroes, paid him only sub-sistence. Because they could find no papers concerning the source of the money, they felt justified, after an interval, in using it for Mary's support.

Huntly is shocked to learn that the rightful owner of the money has appeared. An honest man, he will, of course, see to it that the money is returned; but this act will entail a complete change in his and Mary's plans. Since his parents' deaths at the hands of Indians, Huntly and his sisters have been totally de-pendent on their uncle, whose son, we learn, hates them so much that he will probably turn them out when the farm comes into his hands. Because Huntly has no means to support a wife, he and Mary had expected to live on the money Waldegrave had left; and, after his marriage to Mary, Huntly had planned to provide a refuge in their home for his sisters. Weymouth's arrival, therefore, is a crushing blow to these hopes. Coming on top of his loss of Waldegrave's letters, his feelings of guilt at having preserved them, and his compulsive desire to help Clithero, whom he has in effect driven into the wilderness by prying into his past, this revelation finally forces Huntly over the edge of sanity—a fact that is revealed to the reader in one of the most startling turns of plot to be found in an American novel.

Edgar Huntly abruptly changes direction at this point. The ensuing chapter opens with Huntly in complete darkness, his body aching, and his mind completely disoriented. He does not know where he is nor how he got there, and only gradually does he acquire an understanding of his surroundings. It is obvious to the reader that Huntly is trapped in the cave. He has, if one may take the action figuratively, not only followed Clithero over the bounds of sanity but has also suffered a kind of symbolic death—the first of several that he may be said to experience in the novel.[13] In a passage that reminds one of some of Poe's short tales and of *The Narrative of Arthur Gordon Pym*,[14] Huntly describes his condition at one point: "Sometimes I imagined myself buried alive. Methought I had fallen into seeming death, and my friends had consigned me to the tomb, from which a resurrection was impossible." Such a thought, he tells us, does not terrify him since, he goes on to say, "my state was full of tumult and confusion, and my attention was incessantly divided between my painful sensations and my feverish dreams." Huntly's mind is, at this time, in a "species of delerium." He exists, "as it were, in a wakeful dream" in which "the images of the past occurred in capricious combinations and vivid hues" (IV, 154-55).

IV *Return to Sanity*

Huntly's recovery is only gradual, and his return to sanity is not complete until the end of the book. Slowly, however, he does reorient himself to the physical world. When he first awoke, he writes, his "thoughts were wildering and mazy, and, though consciousness was present, it was disconnected with the locomotive or voluntary power" (IV, 152). But he eventually perceives that his posture is supine, and gradually he rises and feels his way around his prison. Still disoriented, he can locate himself in neither space nor time: "the utter darkness disabled me from

comparing directions and distances" (IV, 154); and he was ex-
cluded from measuring time by his inability to perceive change
in the external world and by his incapacity to gauge it accurately
through "the succession of [his] thoughts" (IV, 155). The cravings of hunger enable him to focus his thinking more sharply; he
then attempts to locate himself by sound, succeeding at last in
identifying his position by the echoes he generates, which re-
semble, "with remarkable exactness" (IV, 155), the sounds he
had previously produced in the cave. Now fully aware of his
precise location, Huntly begins to think rationally of his predicament and to recognize that he has by some mischance fallen into
a pit in the cavern. Properly oriented again in space, he attempts
to extricate himself from his difficulties.

The rest of the book describes Huntly's struggle to return to
normality, but the process is long and difficult and beset with
numerous unforeseen dangers that teach him how little he knows
about his own strengths and weaknesses. Slowly and with great
effort, he makes his way up the sides of the pit, frequently falling back again when the walls become too smooth, but at last
he draws himself painfully over the brink. No sooner does he
arrive at relative safety than he sees two spots of light gleaming
in the darkness, spots that he immediately recognizes as the eyes
of a panther. Fortunately, he has a tomahawk, which, with the
unexpected strength called forth by the desperateness of his situation, he flings at the animal. Recovering from the sinking reaction
he immediately experiences, he feels such pangs of hunger that
he feeds on the carcass of the beast he has killed. So avidly does
he eat that he falls victim to excruciating agonies in his stomach.
At length, his pains subside, and he falls into a deep sleep but is
disturbed by dreams of tantalizing visions of food and drink that
he cannot approach. He awakes less feeble of body, having survived the natural dangers that have assailed him.

In the succeeding action, Huntly encounters new perils; these
derive not so much from the physical environment as from the
passions and errors of men—himself included. To be sure, he
awakes with a burning thirst; but, as he works his way toward
the entrance of the cave, he hears running water with which to
assuage it. What keeps him from rushing to it is the recognition
that a number of Indians are encamped in the mouth of the
cavern, whose warlike intent is revealed by the presence of a
female captive. In a suspenseful series of incidents, Huntly

manages to escape from the cave, and, driven by his great thirst, to overcome his aversion to bloodshed and his childhood fear of Indians derived from his parents' massacre. He kills one of the redskins and even succeeds in making off with the unfortunate captive. His escape from the remaining savages is only tempo- rary; after eating and resting at an abandoned hut in the wilder- ness, he encounters them again and eventually kills all of them. Edgar Huntly thus discovers within himself unforeseen and un- expected resources when his very survival depends upon action, but he also learns that physical weakness can betray him. Ap- proached by a party of whites in pursuit of the savages, Huntly, who had been so strong and capable when danger was imminent, faints away when help arrives. His swoon is mistaken for death,[15] and Huntly revives only to find himself abandoned in the wilderness.

His mind, moreover, continues to play him false; for, con- fronted with certain specific facts, he leaps, as he has done be- fore, to erroneous conclusions. On his escape from the cave, Huntly had hurriedly seized the musket of one of the Indians, but he had had no chance to examine it closely until he arrived at the hut. He is horrified to learn, when he does inspect it, that the musket is his own, the very one given him by Sarsefield and left in the closet of his chamber at his uncle's house. He con- cludes that his "uncle and . . . sisters had been murdered; the dwelling had been pillaged, and this had been a part of the plunder" (IV, 178). Such thoughts of an imagined catastrophe had almost driven him back to the mountain to slaughter the remaining Indians he had left there, a mad intent that is thwarted only by their timely arrival at the hut and their subsequent de- struction at Huntly's hands. When he awakes from his swoon and finds himself once more alone, he struggles back toward Soles- bury, burning with impatience to learn what has become of his family (IV, 203).

Huntly is thus as driven by compulsion to make his way home as he had been to seek Waldegrave's murderer or to pursue Cli- thero in order to help him, and his imprudence almost leads to his destruction. Refreshed at a frontier cabin, he attempts to hurry over a dangerous ridge. He soon loses his way as night is falling. Unable to sleep or to make a fire to protect himself from the icy wind that rises, he contemplates leaping into the river that flows below the cliff; for, once in the water, he could seek

a road along the bank and make his way home. As he prepares
to leap, he hears the sound of human voices, and his fears convince him that Indians are once again near. Lying quietly on the
ground, he sees seven figures pass in the darkness; but an eighth,
coming behind the rest, stops and looks toward him. Fearful that
an Indian could not fail to perceive him even in the darkness,
Huntly jumps to his feet; fires his piece at the shadowy figure;
and, dropping the musket, leaps into the water. There he is
barely missed by the bullets fired after his fleeing figure.[16]
Huntly survives his brush with death and eventually makes his
way along the opposite shore, where new evidence supports his
conviction that his family has been destroyed.

When he approaches a ford in the river, he meets a country
man who informs him of recent events: that Indians had attacked
the settlements and "that one house in Solesbury had been rifled
and burnt on the night before last." Such information only adds
fuel to Huntly's fears; and, since the man does not remember
whose house it was, Huntly's imagination runs riot. "All was
lost!" he writes. "All for whose sake I had desired to live had
perished by the hands of these assassins! That dear home, the
scene of my sportive childhood, of my studies, labours, and rec-
reations, was ravaged by fire and the sword,—was reduced to
a frightful ruin!" He fears that "the means of subsistence itself"
are lost to him by the death of his uncle and by the succession
of his cousin to the farm, and he laments the loss of his books
and possessions. He is comforted to hear that one of the girls
who had been captured by the Indians has been recovered and
immediately believes that this refers to one of his sisters; he
completely forgets that he had himself rescued a captive who was
no relation to him (IV, 224-25). So much have fear, fatigue,
and the memory of his parents' tragedy affected him that he is
incapable of thinking calmly; instead, he rushes madly on his
compulsive way.

Huntly is eventually disabused of his wild errors; for, entering
a house to seek information and help, he runs unexpectedly into
his own packet of Waldegrave's letters and finally into Sarsefield himself, who has arrived in America, visited the Huntly
farm, and, realizing what Huntly has done, located the letters
hidden under the roof. Sarsefield informs him that his uncle is in
fact dead, killed by an Indian who had taken the musket with
which the uncle had armed himself in going out on the expedi-

tion, but the farm and Edgar's sisters are completely safe. Huntly learns that his precipitate action had delayed his own rescue and placed his and Sarsefield's lives in danger; for, in leaving the hut where he had fainted, he had missed Sarsefield, who later came in search of him and found him gone. And, in firing on the imagined Indian on the ridge, he had almost killed his friend, who had likewise almost killed him when he leaped from the cliff. Indeed, Sarsefield himself had twice given Huntly up for dead. Thus, Brown seems to say, are human plans thwarted by chance and circumstances, some external and physical, but others residing in the human being himself, like the fears and compulsions by which Huntly has been madly driven.

Edgar Huntly should realize at this point that his plans and purposes, his desire to do good for others, should be viewed with considerable caution, since so many of his inferences have been proven false and so much of his supposedly benevolent action has led to near disaster for himself and others. He comes to believe, as he writes to Mary, that "the mass of misery and error" in which man is "forever involved" is made "by his own hands"; and he recognizes how mental phantoms had led him to the cave in his sleep and dropped him into the pit. "How little cognizance have men," he concludes, "over the actions and motives of each other! How total is our blindness with regard to our own performances!" (IV, 267). Yet despite his apparent awareness of man's capacity for self-deception and error, particularly in ascertaining the motives of others and in foreseeing the consequences of his own acts, he persists in his desire to help Clithero, even though it was this very purpose which had first led him into the difficulties that he has just barely survived. He still believes that he has judged him correctly and has it within his power to bring him back to normality.

Thus, when Clithero is brought in wounded after having been rescued from Indian captivity, Huntly tries to enlist Sarsefield to help the injured man. Though Sarsefield refuses, he does agree reluctantly that Huntly should tell Clithero that he did not kill Mrs. Lorimer, now Sarsefield's wife, even though Sarsefield does not believe that Clithero's insanity can be cured. Before Huntly can accomplish his purpose, Clithero again escapes to the wilderness. Sarsefield, of course, is anxious to forget about Clithero, but Huntly will not let well enough alone. He seeks him out once again in the hope that by telling him the truth—that Mrs. Sarsefield is alive and well in New York—he may relieve his feelings of guilt and remorse. He is horrified to learn that once Clithero is informed of these facts, he immediately rushes off to seek her out, muttering that his "evil destiny" has reserved him "for the performance of a new crime" (IV, 276). Too late, Huntly realizes that Clithero is indeed a maniac who cannot be recalled to sanity by any power of reason that Huntly possesses. All Huntly can do is to dispatch a letter to New York telling Sarsefield what has happened and urging him to head Clithero off.

Huntly's defense of his actions is highly significant, for it clearly reveals how seriously he has erred in trusting without question his ability to draw just inferences from events, and in acting upon those conclusions. "Yet who could foresee this consequence of my intelligence?" Huntly writes to Sarsefield. "I imagined that Clithero was merely a victim of erroneous gratitude, a slave of the errors of his education and the prejudices of his rank; that his understanding was deluded by phantoms in the mask of virtue and duty, and not, as you have strenuously maintained, utterly subverted." Huntly knows that his own actions must be censured, for he admits that his "unfortunate temerity has created this evil." Nonetheless, he defends himself with the thought that, although he has erred, he did so not "through sinister or malignant intentions, but from the impulse of misguided, indeed, but powerful, benevolence" (IV, 277). His "benevolence" has consequences that are not revealed until Sarsefield's reply to the letter. Clithero has indeed been intercepted, but the terror that Sarsefield's wife experienced on learning that Clithero was approaching caused her to miscarry, the baby died, and Clithero ended his life a suicide.

The book ends at this point with Huntly fully aware of the consequences of his actions. Presumably, he is brought back to sanity at the end of his experience; not only is he able to write the story of his adventures to Mary Waldegrave after most of the events have occurred, but he can also generalize on their meaning. "What light has burst upon my ignorance of myself and of mankind!" he writes. "How sudden and enormous the transition from uncertainty to knowledge!" (IV, 6). To be sure, he expresses this opinion before the final incidents of the story occur, but the dénouement serves only to confirm it.

If one may take his statement, then, as a valid judgment on the intended meaning of Huntly's experience, the novel details his awakening to self-knowledge. He is made to see his madness for what it is and to admit the errors he has fallen into. Even the solution of Waldegrave's murder contributes to Huntly's education, for it reveals how consistently he has failed to interpret events correctly. Waldegrave fell victim to a single Indian, who, arriving with a small band before the main attack, resolved to kill the first person he chanced upon (IV, 269-70). From the very beginning, Huntly had fallen into error in his interpretation of events—an error which led him down the path of conjectures, plans, and compulsions that eventually brought such disastrous results.

V *Thematic Meaning and Literary Value*

Thus, *Edgar Huntly* details the experience of a character who, much like those in *Wieland,* attempts to form just inferences from his perception of the physical world; and, like them, he fails in the attempt. Like Wieland himself, Huntly has fallen under the influence of such strong irrational forces that he is no longer capable of properly estimating his own mental state.[17] Huntly's friendship with Waldegrave and his desire to avenge his friend's death disqualify him as an objective seeker of truth in trying to determine the identity of the murderer; and his abnormal mental condition, paralleling that of the mad Clithero, makes him an unsuitable judge of that unfortunate man. The series of emotional shocks he receives in the course of the narrative and the severe physical and mental strain he undergoes on his return from the cave further affect his ability to think rationally. While the events are taking place, Huntly himself is scarcely aware of his own deficiency; but, relying to the end on his own disturbed mind, he continues to act in the world as if he were in complete control of his reason and were able to foresee clearly the results of the chain of circumstances that he sets in motion.

If Brown in *Edgar Huntly* echoes the critique of the rationalist approach to life that he had made in *Wieland,* he also questions the validity of the emotionalist attitude that Huntly sometimes exhibits. For, although Edgar Huntly believes that Clithero's madness can be cured by the use of reason and the simple statement of the truth that his patroness is not dead (IV, 91, 273), he also feels a powerful sympathy for the man. He observes at one point in the novel that, should his arguments fail, there are other means by which he might manage to help him. Thus, he writes that "to sit by him in silence, to moisten his hand with tears, to sigh in unison, to offer him the spectacle of sympathy, the solace of believing that his demerits were not estimated by so rigid a standard by others as by himself, that one at least among his fellow-men regarded him with love and pity, could not fail to be of benign influence" (IV, 101-2). Though Huntly's own madness and subsequent personal troubles keep him from fulfilling this purpose, it is with a similar emotion of pity and desire "to afford him comfort and inspire him with courage and hope" (IV, 272) that he finally seeks Clithero out in the forest to reveal the presence of Sarsefield's wife in America, with the terrible results that follow.

In Huntly's appeal, moreover, to his own benevolent motives in defense of his final acts and in his interpretation of Clithero's deeds as the result of a "spirit of mistaken benevolence" (IV, 86), Brown also reinforces the critique of benevolist principles that had already appeared in his novels. One is reminded of the various characters in his other books who make similar appeals to explain their deeds: Carwin, who had argued at one point that he was conferring a benefit on the Wielands when in reality he had merely succumbed to his overpowering curiosity and desire to meddle in their affairs; and Ormond, who had used the same plea in his attempt to justify the murder of Stephen Dudley. More closely allied to the view as it appears in *Edgar Huntly* are Arthur Mervyn's professions of benevolent intent at the very moment his actions are helping him toward selfish ends. Since neither Mervyn nor Huntly is presented as a willful villain, each must be seen as a sincere young man whose intent is apparently good, but who, though professing benevolent principles, achieves an end quite different from the one he proposes. It seems obvious from the actions of both these heroes that Brown questions the value of their principles as guides to proper conduct.

Brown makes no attempt, of course, to resolve any of the philosophic questions he raises in the book, nor does he present any alternative values for those which Huntly has professed. Though he does reveal that Huntly still retains, in part at least, the irreligious views that Waldegrave unfortunately instilled in him (IV, 126), not much is made of the matter in the book; and we cannot conclude, as we could with *Ormond*, that Brown suggests the importance of a religious view of the world as the guide to life. We can merely observe that in *Edgar Huntly*,

Brown is content, as he had been in *Arthur Mervyn*, to allow his characters to act out the intellectual drama and to suggest through the obvious contrast between the characters' professions and their practical results in action the serious reservations he apparently maintained concerning the validity of their principles. Although the reader might wish that the book were intellectually more rounded and complete, still he may accept it as an interesting and suspenseful work of fiction and judge it on that basis. Seen in these terms, *Edgar Huntly* will always occupy an important place in the Brown canon and a respectable position in American literature as a whole.

The forward-looking aspects of the novel—the use of the wilderness materials and the savage struggle with the Indians—are enough to secure its place in American literary history. The book deserves better, however, than to be relegated to the limbo of significant but unread books, for it has much to recommend it to the modern reader. Admittedly, there are flaws. The series of events, for example, that establishes the relationship between Huntly and Clithero, though serving a functional purpose in the tale, is difficult for the contemporary reader to accept on the literal level;[18] one cannot really believe in Huntly's mad pursuit of Clithero through the wilderness late at night nor in his repeated attempts to reach him in Norwalk after he has fled there, no matter how much these events may reveal about Huntly's incipient madness. In addition, the sharp contrast in tone between the long retelling of Clithero's past and the exciting adventures of the Indian fighting seriously mars the unity of the tale—as does the stock device of Weymouth's long digression in the middle of the book.

A number of matters are left unresolved at the end of the novel. No provision is made for Huntly's sisters, about whose future he has been so concerned. They are staying at Inglefield's farm when Huntly finally goes in search of Clithero, but no further mention is made of them in the book. We do not learn what happens to Mary Waldegrave, whether she and Huntly ever marry, or what they will manage to live on if they do. Huntly's future, too, is left uncertain when the novel closes; for, though Sarsefield intended to take the young man under his protection, one cannot tell if Huntly's precipitate action, causing as it does a disaster in Sarsefield's family, will affect their future relations. Flaws like these, however, seem more significant when one reflects on the story than they appear to be when the reader is hurried along by the force of events in the suspenseful action. They cannot be completely ignored, and one may regret that Brown did not carry his tale to a neater conclusion. Yet one is inclined to discount their importance in a final judgment of the book because of the obvious strengths which the novel also exhibits.

Foremost among these strengths are the striking effects that Brown creates in the better parts of his book. Few readers, one may suppose, can easily forget such impressive scenes as that when Huntly first sees Clithero digging under the elm, or that in the cave when Huntly—like Poe's protagonist in "The Pit and the Pendulum"[19]—first returns to consciousness and reorients himself to his physical surroundings. Brown was surely as adept as Poe—at least over short passages—in creating the kind of mood that was to characterize the work of his great successor.[20] Few readers, too, can resist the excitement of Huntly's return from the cave, or fail to accord it—bizarre as it is—their general belief. Huntly's experience is a waking nightmare in which incident follows incident at a breath-taking pace, yet the movement itself, one might argue, adds to the reader's conviction; it helps to suggest the compulsion that drives Huntly homeward and thus sustains the melodrama of the events. Not all of the novel can be defended in these terms, nor would one wish to suggest that such passages, memorable as they are, represent the highest degree of literary achievement. On the other hand, their power is undeniable.

More important for the permanent reputation of the novel is the depiction of the hero; Edgar Huntly is characterized with something of the subtlety that makes Arthur Mervyn so unforgettable a character. Both heroes are allowed to tell their own stories, and Brown shows considerable skill in writing speech that reveals to the reader much more than the characters intend. Not that the characterization is obvious. Indeed, Huntly's descent into madness is so skillfully presented that many readers are probably not aware that Huntly is a sleepwalker until rather late in the book;[21] nor, one may suppose, do they perceive at once the series of parallels that Brown draws between Huntly's and Clithero's characters and actions. The methods of characterization are relatively unobtrusive, so that Huntly's true mental state only gradually dawns on the reader while the hero himself generally believes he is acting on rational grounds. The contrast between his thoughts and the reader's opinion of him provides the means through which the character is finally revealed.

Brown's success in depicting the leading character in *Edgar Huntly* is not so great, perhaps, as in *Arthur Mervyn*. The hero of the latter book is by far the more complex and more interesting. His rise to success engages the reader more closely than does Huntly's retreat into madness, for Mervyn represents a type of personality more readily recognizable in the real world. Indeed, the realism of *Arthur Mervyn*—especially the plague episode in the first part—stands in sharp contrast to the dreamlike quality of the other book. Yet *Edgar Huntly* too has its virtues. A book need not be realistic to be enjoyable, and the best parts of *Edgar Huntly* are just as successful for what they do as are the best of *Arthur Mervyn*. The plot line is straighter in *Edgar Huntly*, the point of view is more consistently maintained, and the book has a suspenseful quality that Brown had not equaled since *Wieland*. Taken on balance, *Edgar Huntly* should perhaps be assigned the second position among Brown's novels. Better focused than the rather confused and chaotic *Arthur Mervyn*, it resembles *Wieland* in its effective detail and suspenseful action. In main plot construction and consistency of tone, however, it is inferior to *Wieland*, which, for all its obvious faults, remains Brown's most successful novel.

CHAPTER 6

Minor Novels

WITH THE PUBLICATION of *Edgar Huntly* in the summer of 1799, Brown completed a remarkable year as an author, for most of the work upon which his literary reputation depends had been published within the preceding twelve months. Of his major novels, only part two of *Arthur Mervyn* was yet to appear. Brown was never again to write so prolifically nor so well, but his career as a novelist was by no means over. In addition to the second part of *Arthur Mervyn*, two more novels and a substantial fragment were still to come from his pen, books hardly the equal of the work he had already done, but still worthy of close attention. Of the three, the fragment, *Memoirs of Stephen Calvert*, should be considered first, for much of it seems to have been written between the appearance of *Edgar Huntly* and part two of *Arthur Mervyn*. Brown began its publication in *The Monthly Magazine and American Review* in June, 1799, when he was probably finishing *Edgar Huntly;* and he continued the story in installments until June, 1800, around the time the second part of *Arthur Mervyn* must have been completed. Brown's final novels, *Clara Howard* and *Jane Talbot*, two books written in the sentimental manner, did not appear until 1801.[1]

I Stephen Calvert

Brown had begun to write *Stephen Calvert* in September, 1798. He laid the work aside when he turned to other novels, but he probably took it up again the following spring, writing the episodes, according to Warfel, as they appeared in *The Monthly Magazine* (177). Although *Stephen Calvert* has never been published as a separate volume in this country,[2] it takes up nearly two hundred closely printed pages in Dunlap's biography,[3] and is, in effect, almost a self-contained unit. Brown claimed it was but one part of a projected five-part book (II, 472), and a number of loose ends are left at the close of the tale; but, much like the first part of *Arthur Mervyn*, it can be read as a reasonably complete unit that details the adventures of a young man,[4] who, in this case, retires from society to the shores of Lake Michigan to escape from the "temptation and calamity" of the world, and who tells the story of his life to an interested visitor who has come to his wilderness retreat (II, 274-75).

Calvert begins his tale with an account of his family background in Europe. Calvert's grandfather, Sir Stephen Porter, was an English Catholic who had reared his two sons to be soldiers. The elder, Henry, followed his father's wishes; but the younger, who was exposed to the arguments of a Protestant minister in Flanders and later fell in love with a French Huguenot, renounced both his religion and his profession, and secretly married the girl. Sir Stephen, unaware of his son's apostasy, drew him into a plot to place the Stuarts again on the throne; but the son, assuming his wife's name, Calvert, fled to Pennsylvania, where, suspected by the conspirators of having betrayed the plot, he eventually met a mysterious end.

Before the flight to America, his wife had borne him twin sons, Felix and Stephen. In the course of the complicated process by which the family traveled to America, the twins were separated, and Felix was left with a nurse in England. The boy was abducted by old Sir Stephen; and his parents, who were already in America, fearing him lost to them forever, changed Stephen's name to Felix. This second Felix Calvert is the narrator of the tale.

As the story progresses, young Calvert grows up in America with his widowed mother and inherits an estate from a cruel uncle who has unjustly cast out his daughter, Louisa. Felix, an emotionally unstable boy who worships love and acts on impulse and passion, falls in love with Louisa in his imagination before he even meets her; but he abruptly changes his mind when he sees that she is short, pockmarked, and unattractive. He realizes that in justice the estate should be hers, and even reveals at one point that he intends to give it to her. Yet at the same time, he cannot bring himself to part with it; and, though he does not love her, he even considers proposing marriage, reconciling himself to the idea by dwelling upon her excellent character.

It is obvious to the reader that Felix is rationalizing; he, like Arthur Mervyn, is influenced in his plans for marriage by the thought of material gain. Louisa, on the other hand, does indeed love him; and, when he asks her to marry him, she immediately accepts. Their marriage is blocked by a friend, Sidney Carlton, who loves Louisa himself and who correctly points out to her that the "passionate and headstrong" Felix is as yet too unstable to be a proper partner for her. Convinced by his argument, Louisa insists that the marriage be postponed until his "character is matured by that age and experience in which [he is] now deficient" (II, 337-38, 344).

Sidney is soon proved right in his judgment of Calvert's character, for Felix falls in love with Clelia Neville, whose life he has saved in a fire. Overwhelmed by Clelia's beauty and talent, which stands in sharp contrast to the homely aspect of the plain Louisa, Felix visits her often. But, because he is not yet sure of the lovely Clelia, he does not cut himself off completely from his cousin, nor does he tell her of his love for Clelia. From this point on, Felix becomes increasingly ensnared in the web of deceit he has woven. When, on proposing to her, he learns that Clelia is already married, he turns to his cousin though he has not seen her for a fortnight; and, informed that Sidney and she are aware that he has been courting another woman, he tells Louisa part of the truth and assures her that he will not see Clelia again. Despite his promise, he soon begins to think of Clelia, convinces himself that there may be a reasonable explanation for her behavior, and goes to her when she sends him a letter. Swayed by whichever woman has his ear at the moment, Felix readily accepts her story that she was urged against her will into marriage with a depraved man named Belgrave and has fled to America to escape his cruelty. Indeed, Felix even agrees to become her friend once more and resumes his visits.

Felix is eventually confronted with the possibility that he has been completely duped by the woman's story. For Sidney has learned, Louisa tells Felix, that Belgrave is no monster. Indeed, Clelia is said to be a profligate who retained her father's clerk as a paramour even after her marriage. When Felix goes to Sidney with the demand that he present proof of the charge, Sidney replies that he has it: Clelia is again seeing her lover in America. Felix, on his part, refuses to believe the report since he is certain that Clelia has no visitors but himself; and he and Sidney are soon at odds over the evidence which each thinks he possesses. Sidney reports that Clelia was entertaining her para-

mour the preceding Saturday night; and, when Felix insists that
it could not be true because he was with her at the time, Sidney
believes that Felix is telling a deliberate lie, for *he* thinks that
Felix was seen playing draughts in a tavern at the time. He does
not fully reveal this piece of information, however, and Felix is
dismayed when Sidney and Louisa dismiss him as a lying wretch.
He is further confused when Clelia Neville, asking him questions
about his past which he answers truthfully, also banishes him.

It is apparent to the reader that the other Felix has appeared
on the scene and that the two are so much alike that one is easily
mistaken for the other. The confusion is eventually straightened
out—after a mad trip to sea, near shipwreck, and rescue on Felix's
part—and the story ends just as the brothers are at the point of
meeting. Brown is thus using the ancient device of unrecognized
twins to ring a variation upon the theme of *Wieland*: the ease
with which the senses may be deluded to lead even the best
disposed persons, like Sidney Carlton,[5] to erroneous conclusions;
but in *Stephen Calvert* it is sight, not hearing, which is deceived.
The device, however, does not work nearly so well in this story,
for certain serious difficulties obtrude. If Felix and Stephen are
really so different in appearance as both Clelia and Sidney
eventually recognize, one wonders how Clelia could have mistaken one for the other.[6] Indeed, if Clelia and the real Felix
actually carried on an affair in Europe as they are reported to
have done, it is inconceivable that she and Felix-Stephen could
have established the kind of relationship described in the novel.
Surely some reference to the past by Clelia would have enlightened him or at least have made him suspicious.

The theme of deceptive appearance is not the main one in the
novel, but rather the errors of imposture and self-deception into
which an impetuous youth, like Felix Calvert, is led by following
impulse and passion.[7] The point Brown makes with his hero is
a good one, and the action develops the theme in a rather convincing manner. Yet one may well question whether the character of the young man is not really too simple to sustain for
long a major work of fiction. Felix's vacillations are interesting
only up to a point. Transparent as he is, he lacks the complexity—
and indeed the subtlety of presentation—that engages the reader's
interest in Arthur Mervyn and in Edgar Huntly, the heroes of
Brown's books that he resembles most.[8] Granted the character
and the fullness of the thematic development, it is difficult to see

where the story might still have gone; for, by the end of the fragment, the point of the tale has been thoroughly made. This is not to say that the novel has no virtues—the characterization of the plain but honest, and, in her own way, attractive Louisa, is a major one—but it is probably just as well that Brown did not attempt to finish the story.

With the abandonment of *Stephen Calvert* and with the completion of *Arthur Mervyn* in 1800, the major phase of Brown's career as a novelist was over, and many changes in both his life and his writing were soon to occur. The end of the year brought the conclusion of the third and last volume of *The Monthly Magazine,* a periodical which continued for two more years as a quarterly, renamed *The American Review and Literary Journal,* but with which Brown seems to have had little close connection.[9] Late in 1800, Brown returned to Philadelphia to live with his brother James and to join both James and Armitt in their importing business.[10] Other changes too were in the making. Before he left New York, Brown had fallen in love with Elizabeth Linn, whom he was to marry in 1804. Indeed, even the direction of Brown's work took a new turn since the books he published in 1801 make a sharp departure from the kind of work he had done in his most important fiction. Both *Clara Howard* and *Jane Talbot* are sentimental tales of love and marriage.

Brown was aware that the highly unusual incidents that had characterized a work like *Edgar Huntly* laid him open to criticism, for he had written his brother James in April, 1800, that although James's "remarks upon the gloominess and out-of-nature incidents of Huntley [*sic*]" were perhaps "not just in their full extent," they were, "doubtless, such as most readers will make." This alone, he goes on to say, "is a sufficient reason for dropping the doleful tone and assuming a cheerful one, or, at least substituting moral causes and daily incidents in place of the prodigious or the singular. I shall not fall hereafter into that strain."[11] Such a decision, of course, can only be regretted, for Brown, in making this resolve, turned his back upon the kind of fiction in which he had achieved his greatest success. What he finally wrote in place of it can hardly be called an improvement; for *Clara Howard* and *Jane Talbot* are undoubtedly his poorest novels. The books are not total failures, inasmuch as Brown managed to instill some narrative drama and intellectual interest into almost everything he wrote. But the sentimental style was not his forte, and the epistolary device he chose for the development of both novels brought the action to a virtual standstill. Some of his old power remains, but only on occasion does it break through the sentimental tone of the letters.

II Clara Howard

The shortest of Brown's novels, *Clara Howard; or, The Enthusiasm of Love* is surely also the weakest; for, although it reminds the reader of both *Arthur Mervyn* and *Stephen Calvert*, it projects its theme through an action that one finds hard to accept. In the story, Philip Stanley, a poor country lad, has gained the affection of a cultivated English gentleman, Mr. E. Howard, who tutors him for a while but suddenly departs for Europe, apparently never to return. When Philip goes to the city to become a watchmaker's apprentice, he meets Mary Wilmot, a rather homely girl nine years his senior who had been reared in luxury, but who, now fallen on evil days, supports her brother and herself by sewing. Despite the difference in age, she falls in love with him, but Philip does not return her love. Nevertheless, he does consider marriage with her. Totally inexperienced with women and admiring her many good qualities, he does not realize that he may one day feel more strongly toward another. When, at her brother's death, Mary comes unexpectedly into an inheritance of five thousand dollars, Philip becomes importunate that they marry; and Mary finally consents, believing that the benefit she can bestow on him with her money will compensate him for a loveless marriage. She defers the ceremony for half a year, however, so that he can be certain that he wants to go through with it.

Before that time elapses, a man named Morton appears to claim the brother's money, and Howard returns unexpectedly with a wife and beautiful stepdaughter, Clara. Now quite wealthy, Howard takes Philip into his house as his son. Mary, naturally, is deeply affected by the news. Believing that her money is lost and that Philip will fare better with the young, beautiful, wealthy Clara, Mary disappears with a man named Sedley and his sister, Mrs. Valentine. She sends a letter to Philip, which is misplaced at his country home and does not come into his hands until four months later. Thus unaware of what has become of Mary, Philip considers his engagement broken and turns his attention to Clara; but, when he tells her of his previous betrothal to Mary, she reacts in an unexpected manner.

Full of benevolist desire to make other people happy, Clara insists that it is his duty to find Mary and to marry her if her happiness demands it. She is convinced that she can never be happy herself if her joy must be bought by Mary's unhappiness. Therefore, although she too loves Philip, she refuses to marry him while Mary is single and unhappy. She even demands that he persuade Mary to marry him and offers them half her fortune so that she—Clara—can enjoy the pleasure of sacrificing herself to another's happiness![12]

Philip is thus presented with an absurd situation, forced by the woman he loves to find and perhaps marry one he does not love and who has disappeared without a trace. But he does what Clara demands, and he eventually finds Mary's misplaced letter. So full is it of heartbreak and threats of dying because of the calamity which has befallen her that Philip resolves at first to go through with the proposal. Thoughts of Clara deter him, and he finally decides to find Mary and restore the money, which, he has recently learned, Morton will not claim. Before he can perform this duty, Philip falls sick with a fever, contracted while saving a girl from drowning, and lies near death. Clara, horrified at the thought that he might die, relents in the demands she has made and summons him back to her, though not without some fears that she is doing an injustice to Mary. Philip is overjoyed at the news but wants first to find Mary and to restore her funds to her. Clara, however, runs into Mary at the house of an acquaintance. Without even asking her condition, she assumes that she is still single and unhappy, and she demands once again that Philip persuade her to marry him.

What neither Philip nor Clara knows is that Mary's condition has changed. She has learned from Mrs. Valentine, with whom she has been staying, that the five thousand dollars is really hers, the gift of Sedley, who has long loved Mary and who had used the roundabout means of helping her by sending the sum anonymously to her brother. Impressed by his generosity—he knew the money might be used to support her and Philip—Mary begins at last to feel affection for him. Convinced by Mrs. Valentine, whose name is surely significant, of the folly of longing for one who does not return her affection, she finally agrees to marry Sedley. Before Philip learns Mary's decision, he rushes to propose to her, for he has become convinced that Clara cannot love him and act the way she does. He goes through a period of torment when it looks as if neither girl will have him: Clara, because she thinks Mary is unhappy; Mary, because she has renounced him to Clara. Caught in the middle and hurrying away from Mary before she has a chance to explain her new plans, Philip resolves, like Stephen Calvert, to disappear into the wilderness. But, before he has hardly started, he conveniently falls sick on the way, and letters catch up with him to reveal the truth: that Mary will marry Sedley and be happy. The impediment thus removed, Clara welcomes him with open arms, and the book ends with plans being made for two weddings.

It is difficult for the modern reader to take such a story seriously since the problem that the characters face is essentially an artificial one that could be solved by the application of a little common sense. One cannot really believe the absurd vacillations that the characters go through when the solution to their difficulties is so obvious. In style, the book is little better; it descends at times to the kind of overwrought emotionalism typical of the sentimental novel, with Philip even writing a passage like the following: "Why do I write? For whose use do I pass my time thus? There is no one living who cares a jot for me. There was a time when a throbbing heart, a trembling hand, and eager eyes were always prepared to read and ruminate on the scantiest and poorest scribble that dropped from my pen: but she has disappeared; the veil between us is like death" (VI, 289). In form, too, the novel is weak. Too much of the action is simply summarized in a long letter that takes up nearly a fourth of the book, and far too little happens in the rest of it. The complications of the plot—the misplaced letter and the two convenient illnesses that Philip contracts during the course of the story—are trite and contrived.

Brown also made the mistake in *Clara Howard* of repeating situations and incidents that he had already used in *Edgar Huntly*. Thus, Philip Stanley, like Huntly, lives with an uncle who supports him and his sisters, but whose son has developed such an implacable enmity toward them that they will be cast off the farm when his father dies (VI, 323). Philip and Mary, like Huntly and Mary Waldegrave in the earlier novel, depend for their future on a mysterious sum of money left by the girl's dead brother. Wilmot, like Waldegrave, courts poverty while doing good to others; and Morton, like Weymouth, consigns a sum of money to his friend before being shipwrecked on the other side of the Atlantic. Details differ, of course, in the two incidents, and the claim in *Clara Howard* turns out to be false. But the use again of such a device can hardly add to the stature of Brown as a novelist—nor can the materials themselves be said to strengthen a novel that is already seriously weak.

Yet *Clara Howard* should not be dismissed without further attention, for the book is not without interest, limited though its merits may be. One might well make a mistake, for example, if he took the actions of the characters at their face value. The careful reader will note that here, as in *Arthur Mervyn*, there is a strange contradiction between the characters' acts and their professions of principle. Thus Clara Howard insists that reason alone must guide their actions, that rationality demands both the sacrifice of her happiness to Mary's and Philip's willing performance of the duty she lays upon him; but the action of the book indicates that she is no more immune to emotionalism than the others. One wonders, for example, whether the ultimate reason for the demands she makes on Philip does not derive in part from an emotional identification with Mary's plight, since she believes it is her duty "to judge of the feelings of others by her own" (VI, 347). Clara knows, moreover, the pleasures of both wealth and love, so that she can imagine—she tells Philip at one point—what it would be like to lose both, as Mary has (VI, 351-52). Her sympathy for what she thinks are Mary's sufferings seems to be at least one important influence in motivating her to act as she does.

Nor is this the only incident in which Clara gives way to her emotions. When she first sends Philip off to seek the unfortunate Mary, she is adamant in demanding that he do what she prescribes. He must "zealously solicit" a union with Mary or else be unworthy of her love and esteem, and he must not imagine that any appeal to her sympathy or pity will lead her to change her mind (VI, 302). But, when Philip falls seriously ill and almost dies, Clara forgets all her firm resolutions and begs him to come to her: "The arms of thy Clara are open to receive thee. She is ready to kneel to thee for pardon; to expiate her former obduracy by tears of gratitude and tenderness. Lay on my past offenses what penalty thou wilt: the heavier it be, the more cheerfully shall I sustain it; the more adequate it will be to my fault" (VI, 312). Clara's new resolutions last only a little while. No sooner does she meet Mary than she assumes without asking that Mary is still unhappy; and, apparently as the result of her emotional reaction on seeing the girl, she makes her absurd demands on Philip a second time. None of these actions is the result of a rational choice.

In the light of such evidence, we cannot assume that Clara Howard is a force of reason or of rational duty in the novel—nor can we conclude with David Lee Clark that she is "Brown's ideal woman," or a "humanized Constantia Dudley" (182).[13] She seems, on the contrary, to be merely another of Brown's mistaken benevolists who does not recognize the emotional basis of her actions. Indeed, her error is obvious even to Philip himself, who, although sometimes called rash and impetuous by both Mary and Clara, actually writes her quite sensibly (after she makes her second demands on him) that she is utterly wrong in the decision she has made. In a carefully reasoned letter, he makes the point that her "judgment . . . is misguided." It is absurd, he argues, for Clara to believe that she can secure Mary's happiness by urging him to marry her; because, even if Mary should consent to the union (an event that is not very likely), only unhappiness could come to her from an unloving husband. Besides, Philip goes on to say, Clara acts as if Mary alone is worthy of benevolent treatment, that only Mary's wishes and not his are to be at all considered (VI, 377-79). In this letter, Philip talks sense to Clara, and he emerges as a believable character to the extent that he does so.

Moreover, Philip continues, Clara is acting unjustly. After all, Philip has the same claim on Clara's affections as Mary on his, so that if he is "cruel and unjust in refusing [his] love to one that claims it," then so is Clara in refusing to give her love to him, because "the rule is fallacious that is not applicable to all others in the same circumstances." Besides, Mary and he are not the only ones affected by her decision; Sedley has precisely the same claim on Mary's affections as Mary has on Philip's. "For him and for me," Philip writes, "your benevolence sleeps; with regard to us, you have neither consideration nor humanity; they are all absorbed in the cause of one whose merits, whose claim to your sympathy and aid, if it be not less, is far from being greater, than Sedley's or mine" (VI, 380). Thus, Philip makes clear to Clara that he thinks her completely wrong in her estimate of where her duty lies.

Yet Philip's very rationality in the reply he makes to Clara causes a problem in interpretation; for, if his estimate of Clara's error is as just as it seems, why, one may ask, does he submit to what she calls her better judgment at the end of the book? When Clara summons him back to her in the closing pages, she soundly berates him for planning to go West, and she argues that he must return to her and make her forget his errors "by the rectitude of [his] future conduct" (VI, 404). Philip replies that he will hurry to her at once and asks her forgiveness. At this point we may assume that Philip is motivated by his love for her; but, when he accepts without a murmur the assumption of leadership on the part of one whose judgment in an important matter he has already shown to be in error, one wonders what possesses him. Clara is determined to lead in the marriage. "My maturer age and more cautious judgment," she writes to him, "shall be counsellors and guides to thy inexperienced youth. While I love thee and cherish thee as a wife, I shall assume some of the prerogatives of an elder sister, and put my circumspection and forethought in the balance against thy headlong confidence." She believes that his genius and knowledge will enable him to surpass her in the not very distant future; but, for the time being at least, she claims "to be more than equal" to him "in moral discernment." And the implication is strong that she expects him to conform to her views (VI, 408-9).

Why Philip will accept her under these conditions is hard to understand, but accept her he does without a demur. Thus, the conflict between his actions here and his earlier estimate of her erroneous judgment must somehow be reconciled unless one wishes to dismiss his conduct as utterly inconsistent or as hopelessly confused by romantic love. Brown does present the reader with a few clues which may provide an answer, for there is some evidence to suggest that Philip Stanley—like Arthur Mervyn or, indeed, Stephen Calvert when he first wooed Louisa—is at least as much interested in the money as he is in the girl.[14] Thus, in one of his letters to Clara during the time when they are reconciled, he takes note of her wealth, making it quite plain that, although he would like to be a "universal benefactor," he does not aspire to the control of her money. Since, knowing his own frailty, he trembles at the power of wealth, he will leave it all in her more capable hands. It shall be his glory and boast, he writes, not to seek power over others but "to submit to one whom I deem unerring and divine. Clara's will is my law" (VI, 359-61)! This may, of course, be simply lover's hyperbole. But, because he submits to her will when her wealth is available, and talks back to her most strongly and sensibly when it looks as if it is lost to him, one may well question the purity of his motives.

Other evidence in the book seems to indicate that Philip is interested in a wife with money. He first becomes really determined to wed Mary when she inherits the five thousand dollars from her brother; and, after Mary disappears, he quickly transfers his attention to the more beautiful—and richer—Clara, only to turn once again to Mary when Clara seems lost to him. Indeed, even the Introduction to the book points in the same direction, for Philip writes to a friend to tell him his good fortune at having acquired a wealthy wife and sends the packet of letters that make up the book. This passage deserves full quotation:

> You once knew me a simple lad, plying the file and tweezers at the bench of a watchmaker, with no prospect before me but of labouring, for a few years at least, as a petty and obscure journeyman, at the same bench where I worked five years as an apprentice. I was sprung from obscurity, destitute of property, of parents, of paternal friends; was full of that rustic diffidence, that inveterate humility, which are alone sufficient to divert from us the stream of fortune's favours.
>
> Such was I three years ago! Now I am rich, happy, crowned with every terrestrial felicity, in possession of that most exquisite of all blessings,—a wife, endowed with youth, grace, dignity, discretion.
>
> I do not, on second thoughts, wonder at your curiosity. It was impossible for me to have foreseen, absurd to have hoped for, such a destiny. All that has happened was equally beyond my expectations and deservings [VI, 287-88].

This statement has something of the sound of Arthur Mervyn, who managed to place himself in a similar position of wealth, and suggests that Philip Stanley too may have a bit of the opportunist in his make-up.

Such an interpretation demands that a strain of irony be seen as running through the book; and one must be cautious, as has already been observed, in seeing Brown as a conscious ironist.

Nonetheless, the alternative is to read *Clara Howard* as a very poor piece of sentimental fiction with an absurd action designed merely to illustrate, in an echo of *Stephen Calvert*, the "enthusiasm"—in the eighteenth-century sense—of those in love. Certainly, much of the action of the book can be explained in these terms, and the characters of Philip Stanley and, more especially, Clara Howard bear some resemblance to that of the emotionally volatile Calvert. Philip, however, gives evidence of a calm rationality that Calvert did not possess, and the book contains a strong suggestion of irony that is not apparent in the fragment. Philip's similarity to Arthur Mervyn is so very striking that one is reluctant to see the "enthusiasm of love" as the sole meaning of the book.[15]

This issue is not a very important one. At best, the novel is weak in plotting, tone, and style, so that it will not help very much to see the book as an inferior *Arthur Mervyn*. Brown, after all, had already done the same thing better; and one could hardly recommend a pallid imitation—if such it is—when the much superior *Arthur Mervyn* is available. Even when seen in the most favorable light, *Clara Howard* has little to recommend it to the modern reader.

III Jane Talbot

Jane Talbot, on the other hand, remains of interest even today. Although it resembles the earlier book in its sentimental subject matter and method of presentation, it develops a far more important theme. As in *Clara Howard*, the central concern of the plot is the fundamental problem of sentimental fiction—suitable marriage for the heroine—and the epistolary technique through which the story is told renders the novel almost as static as its predecessor.

Yet *Jane Talbot* is a much more significant book. The problem of intellectual and religious incompatibility that Henry Colden and Jane Talbot confront is certainly more serious than any faced by Philip Stanley and Clara Howard, and the actions of Colden and Jane are considerably more believable. The theme of *Jane Talbot*, too, is a lot more meaningful; the book both comes to grips with problems that had always deeply concerned Brown and finally resolves them. Indeed, the whole movement of the novel illustrates unmistakably that Brown had not lost the power to instill intellectual interest into his fiction, for serious ideas inform this sentimental tale of love no less than they do his major Gothic romances.

The plot itself is a simple one. Jane Talbot, a young widow, is in love with Henry Colden; but their marriage is opposed first by Mrs. Fielder, Jane's adopted mother who has reared her since childhood, and later by Colden's father. The grounds for objection are serious. Mrs. Fielder has seen some letters that Colden had written to a friend named Thomson which reveal that he has been arguing vigorously in favor of the radical doctrine expounded in Godwin's *Political Justice*. He has shown himself to be "the advocate of suicide; a scoffer at promises; the despiser of revelation, of Providence and a future state; an opponent of marriage"; and a defender of sexual enormities. In addition, he feels it incumbent upon him as a duty "to preach with vehemence, his new faith." Indeed, so strong had his belief in the new ideas become that "the rage for making converts seized him; and that Thomson was not won over to the same cause proceeded from no want of industry in Colden" (V, 70-71). The hero of the book, therefore, would seem to be a radical thinker of the school we are already familiar with, in general, from its appearance in other works by Brown.

Mrs. Fielder has reason to believe that Jane has already been strongly influenced by Colden's radical views, and she has seen evidence to convince her that Colden has even induced Jane to put them into practice. For Lewis Talbot, Jane's husband, had, before his death, shown Mrs. Fielder a letter which Jane had supposedly written to Colden and which would clearly indicate— were not part of it a forgery—that Jane and Colden had fallen into adultery. It seems that one night while Talbot was away on business, Colden had visited Jane; and, a severe storm arising, he had been allowed to spend the night under her roof. The following day Jane had begun a letter to Colden, mentioning the fact that he had stayed the night, but the letter was stolen before she had had a chance to finish it. And the thief forged a conclusion which can only be construed as proving their supposed guilt. Because Colden is known to have radical views, Mrs. Fielder lends credence to the letter, believes in Jane's fall, and urges her not to marry her "seducer" lest he drag her further down to sin and shame.

Most of the story, as one would expect, is concerned with the revelation of these events through the letters the characters write.

Mrs. Fielder, in New York, urges Jane, who lives in Philadelphia, to return to her. Meanwhile, Colden, who is visiting the dying Thomson in Wilmington, writes to Jane, urging his love and sincerity. He eventually reveals that he no longer holds the views attributed to him. Jane, torn between love and duty, vacillates between the two; and the story in effect stands still while the characters discuss their problem in long letters. Eventually, the problems are all resolved in favor of the lovers. Colden discovers that the forger is a Miss Jessup, who loved Talbot and sought to estrange him from his wife. She confesses the deed in a letter to Colden, which she later denies as a forgery; and Mrs. Fielder, who accepts her assertion that Colden forged the confession, considers his supposed act as yet another proof of his depravity. Jane and Colden are separated soon thereafter, when he goes to sea. While he is gone, Miss Jessup makes a deathbed confession; and Mrs. Fielder, learning the truth of her daughter's innocence, asks forgiveness for having doubted her. When Colden finally returns, he and Jane are free to marry.

Described thus baldly, the novel would seem to be a conventional sentimental tale, completely different from the original work that Brown had done in his four major books. *Jane Talbot*, however, has something more to offer the modern reader than the marriage problem of Jane and Colden, which is of only secondary interest in the book. More important are the questions Brown raises on the strengths and limitations of reason and emotion as guides to life, and the discussion he includes on the value of religious faith as the foundation for proper behavior. These issues had been important ones in Brown's earlier fiction, for he had questioned radical rationalist views in a number of his books, and in *Ormond* he had even suggested the need for a religious view of life to counter such opinions. Now at last, at the end of his brief career as a novelist, he answers the questions he had previously raised and brings both his intellectual quest and his career to a close.[16]

Brown is doing more in *Jane Talbot* than writing a love story. Jane Talbot and Henry Colden, the reader soon perceives, have intellectual as well as romantic roles to play in the novel, and their final union represents the resolution of a real philosophic question. Colden represents the rationalist view, which, once it has infected the individual, leads him away from religious faith and turns him into a skeptic. Colden has indeed, as Mrs. Fielder believes, fallen under the influence of Godwin's thought. Experience, however, has made him question the validity of Godwin's views, but he still remains something of a rationalist who cannot accept, though he does not oppose, religious faith. Jane considers his "propensity to reason" as one of his faults (V, 137), and would like him to show more signs of emotion. She believes he needs "a little more impetuosity and fervour" in his love. He is "not quite passionate enough," she tells him. "Love has not banished discretion, or blindfolded your sagacity" (V, 54). Even in loving Jane, he maintains control of his reason; and, in general, he provides a balance to the more volatile Jane.

She is precisely the opposite. "I am very far from being a wise girl," she writes in the first line of the novel, and much of what ensues supports her opinion. Indeed, the first incidents she relates, her early life with her father and brother, serve only to confirm it. After her mother's death and her adoption by Mrs. Fielder, Jane's father retired from business; and Jane was horrified to see her brother, Frank, unrestrained by a weak and overly lenient father, spend his own money foolishly, embezzle and waste sums intended for a cousin, and wheedle from his parent not only the income from his investments but even the capital itself. It is apparent to all—and not least to Jane—that Frank, hopelessly corrupted by riotous living, is insatiable in his desire for money. When, all other sources having been exhausted, he approaches Jane herself and asks for the loan of five hundred dollars from a legacy she possesses, she is well aware what her answer should be. "I harboured not a moment's doubt as to the conduct it became me to pursue" (V, 28); and, when he persists with his importunities, she asserts her determination not to part with her money (V, 31).

Despite her knowledge of her brother's character and her good resolutions, Jane eventually relents when he appeals repeatedly to her emotions; for her heart, she writes, "is the sport, the mere plaything, of gratitude and pity. Kindness will melt my firmest resolutions in a moment" (V, 32). Although Jane does not give in at the first appeal to her sympathy, she is incapable of resisting his pleas for long. Eventually she begins to think that she is being too cautious, that her brother really does need her help; and, when he finally looks at her with deep distress in his face, she begs his forgiveness and gives him the money he asks—only to regret the act immediately. Such emotionalism and irresolution are basic to Jane's character; and, despite the fact that she learns the sum was wasted, she lends him money twice more—and almost succumbs a fourth time before her mother takes matters into her own hands and drives Frank away. Mrs. Fielder has thus had ample opportunity to observe the "impetuosity of feeling which distinguished [Jane's] early age" (V, 69), a sensibility which, she believed, required "strict government" (V, 66).

Convinced that Jane must be protected against her own temperament, Mrs. Fielder urged her into a loveless marriage with a somewhat stolid man almost twice her age. That Jane was not cured of her emotionalism by this marriage is testified to by her strong attraction to Colden after her husband's death and by her inability to resist the opposite emotional pulls of either Colden or Mrs. Fielder. Even as a grown woman and widow, Jane is unable to form a resolution and stick to it in the face of appeals to feelings. At the urging of Mrs. Fielder, she vows "an eternal separation from Colden" (V, 78); yet, a word from him destroys her determination. "No will, no reason, have I of my own," she writes (V, 92), a judgment confirmed by Colden himself, who, when she renounces him a second time, observes to his brother-in-law: "There are but two persons in the world who command her affections. Either, when present, (the other absent or silent,) has absolute dominion over her" (V, 151). Rather than continue the struggle for Jane's allegiance, Colden accepts his dismissal, embarks upon a long voyage to the Pacific, and leaves Jane completely under the dominance of Mrs. Fielder.

But, although Jane Talbot is—like Stephen Calvert and, to a certain extent, Clara Howard—primarily a creature of emotion throughout most of the novel, she is indirectly influenced to more rational views by her experience with Henry Colden. Jane has apparently always been a deeply religious person, and she had even objected at first to marrying Talbot because, although he was a good man in his personal conduct, he lacked ardor and conviction in his religious belief and practice. Jane possesses the fervor that was wanting in her husband; but, until she meets Colden, she does not seem to have considered the rational grounds for her belief. When she attempts to lead Colden back to faith, she is shocked to discover that she has no foundation for her principles. Once aware of this fact, she "instantly set [herself] to the business of inquiry," for she suddenly realized that she could not influence his convictions if she did not know the basis for her own. She was aware that she ran a risk in arguing with an unbeliever intellectually stronger than she; but she did not fall prey to his delusions. Rather, she thinks, her "belief is stronger than it ever was" because of her experience (V, 134-36).

While Jane is finding a rational basis for her piety, she also learns an important lesson about human beings. Before she had met Colden, she had followed Mrs. Fielder in considering every unbeliever a black-hearted wretch to be scorned and avoided. She had not thought it possible to love such a person, yet she quickly learns that although she may still "regard unbelief as the blackest stain, as the most deplorable calamity that can befall a human creature," she may nonetheless still love the man as a human being. Her love brings with it the obligation to "rescue him from this calamity" (V, 131-32). Jane, in a sense, is humanized by this perception in a way that Mrs. Fielder is not until the end of her life when she asks forgiveness. For Jane ceases to "hold in scorn or abhorrence those who differ from [her]." Instead, she writes: "I find it possible for men to disbelieve and yet retain their claims to our reverence, our affection, and especially our good offices" (V, 136). In short, though she still condemns his error, she does not hate or revile the man who commits it, for he still has a claim to her respect for his humanity.[17]

Just as Jane is brought to more humane and more rational views as a result of her acquaintance with Colden, so also is he led toward faith by Jane and the others he associates with in the story. The change, however, is not sudden, nor is it initiated by them. He had already moved away from his radical opinions by the time the action of the novel begins, so that Jane's influence only confirms a step he has himself taken. As Jane writes to him at one point, his "own experience had half converted [him] already"; and a closer look at the theories which had ensnared him showed "flaws and discords" which led him to abandon the radical extreme (V, 135). Thus, "you err," she observes, "but are not obstinate in error. If your opinions be adverse to religion, your affections are not wholly estranged from it. Your understanding dissents, but your heart is not yet persuaded to refuse" (V, 133). At this stage of his intellectual development, he is ready to listen to Jane with "unprejudiced attention"—indeed, even with a bias in favor of her opinions (V, 135); and, although it is by no means Jane alone who converts him, she is certainly instrumental in helping him when others, like Mrs. Fielder, would have cast him aside without a hearing.

Of great, if not equal, importance is the influence of Colden's friend Thomson, whom he had once tried to convert to disbelief. Colden is in Wilmington at his dying friend's side when we first meet him, for Thomson had summoned him "to urge ... the truths of religion, at a time when his own conduct might visibly attest their value." Though Thomson suffers much, Colden notes that "his closing hour is serene. His piety now stands him in some stead." Colden insists that he is not so much the enemy of Thomson's views as his friend seems to think (V, 108); and, as he later writes, he listens attentively to Thomson's "arguments and admonitions ... with a suitable spirit." Colden does not think him wrong. Indeed, he goes on to say, "at any time I should have allowed infinite plausibility and subtlety to his reasonings, and at this time I confessed them to be weighty." Because he is deeply concerned about his friend's death and about the uncertainty of his relation to Jane, he makes no immediate decision as to their truth but treasures them for future thought (V, 203).

His opportunity for thinking comes when he goes on his long journey to the Pacific, a voyage he embarks upon because his doubts remain. Thomson's sister, Harriet, advises him to stay away from Jane because Mrs. Fielder's objections to him are not "without just grounds." As Harriet points out to him, any change in his views "must necessarily be slow and gradual," and time might eventually remove the obstacles that stand in the way of their marriage (V, 207-8). Colden is gone longer than he expects, however. Because of a mutiny on board the vessel, he is put ashore on a desert island and is eventually taken to Japan by some fishermen. Before he can make his way home again by way of Batavia and Hamburg, four years have elapsed and a radical change has taken place in his intellectual development. "The incidents of a long voyage," he writes to his brother-in-law on his return, "the vicissitudes through which I have passed, have given strength to my frame, while the opportunities and occasions for wisdom which these have afforded me have made *my mind whole*. I have awakened from my dreams of doubt and misery, not to the cold and vague belief, but to the living and delightful consciousness, of every tie that can bind man to his Divine Parent and Judge" (V, 234).

Although Colden does not detail the steps through which he

ed to have been printed in this order.[7] Both
al a strong concern with political and reli-
more so than do any of Brown's novels; but,
the pieces is generally conservative, Brown
r against any of the systems presented. He
he mask of objective chronicler throughout.
imaginary history, which may indicate, as
the direction of Brown's thinking in his later
are not without interest. The confused state
n the other hand, precludes their being given
on accorded Brown's major fiction.

ng that Brown did in the last years of his life
literary. Between 1803 and 1809, he issued a
al pamphlets on important issues of the day; in
ed a translation of Volney's *A View of the Soil
he United States;* and in 1805 he published the
ife and Character of John Blair Linn"—his wife's
d died the previous year—as an introduction to
inn's poem *Valerian.*

ks, only the pamphlets deserve particular mention.
ished in January, 1803, reveals American concern
ect of French control of Louisiana. Word had got
secret treaty, Spain had ceded the territory to
anger the United States faced once France should
n was brought home to Americans when, in Octo-
panish official at New Orleans withdrew the right
merican traders had enjoyed at that port. Since
ericans relied on the Mississippi River to export their
a powerful nation as France could choke off that
ll and would always pose a threat to the Western
*Address to the Government of the United States on
of Louisiana to the French,* Brown stressed the im-
il by using a literary device. Assuming the *persona* of
ounselor of state, Brown wrote what purported to be
t addressed to Napoleon on the value of Louisiana
dvantages that could accrue to France from its posses-
his point thus made, Brown had only to conclude by
out as an American to urge that the United States act
e the impending threat.

pamphlet that quickly followed in March—*Monroe's
; or, The Conduct of the Government in Relation to Our*

has gone in achieving his newly won faith, he does make clear
to his brother-in-law that this change is permanent. He hopes by
his conduct to be as good an example to others as some have been
to him, and he believes that "indefatigable zeal and strenuous
efforts are indeed incumbent on [him] in proportion to the extent
of [his] past misconduct and the depth of [his] former degen-
eracy" (V, 234). His return to faith has brought him close to
Jane in fundamental belief so that their long-delayed marriage
can now take place. When it occurs, the union of Jane and
Colden will represent the meeting on a kind of middle ground
of the two approaches to life which they have represented in the
book; for, just as Jane's experience saves her from the extremes
of emotionalism and vacillation, so also does Colden's retrieve
him from the rationalism of his former life. Head and heart—in
an anticipation of Hawthorne and Melville[18]—will thus be united
when Jane and Colden wed.

It is not only Hawthorne and Melville whose works are foreshadowed in this book, since *Jane Talbot* bears an even stronger
relation to two of Cooper's novels. Henry Colden's return to
faith as the result of a distant voyage looks forward to Roswell
Gardiner's similar experience in Cooper's *The Sea Lions*, and the
problem of lovers divided by a difference in religious belief appears as well in *The Wing-and-Wing.* Unlike Cooper, Brown
does not mark out the steps in Colden's religious development,
nor does he detail in any concrete way the nature of his belief.
With Cooper, the issue involved was always entirely clear. In
The Wing-and-Wing, the separated lovers are atheist and Roman
Catholic and remain inevitably apart; in *The Sea Lions*, Gardiner
returns to the Trinitarian faith of his sweetheart after having
denied the divinity of Christ. Brown is not so specific in his
development of the theme, and one can level the charge against
his conclusion that the religious faith affirmed is so vague as to
obscure, to some extent, the conflict between the lovers, which
in Cooper's works was always precisely defined.

Despite the importance of *Jane Talbot*, however, both in the
development of Brown's thought and in foreshadowing some
important themes in subsequent writers, the novel is not an
especially good piece of fiction; for the issues are not so well
dramatized as were those in Brown's earlier books. Most of the
character development has already taken place before the novel
opens; the issues are merely discussed rather than acted out by

the characters; and the most important part of the novel—Colden's conversion in the Pacific—is merely summarized briefly in the last few pages of the book. The plot line, moreover, is thin and sentimental; and one soon tires of the weak devices of forged letters and deathbed confessions that motivate the main incidents in the story. To be sure, the novel has considerable unity—more than do most of Brown's better works—but the action is static. Brown elects to tell what has occurred through the letters of his characters rather than to project it through the action of the tale. *Jane Talbot* thus strikes the modern reader as a wordy book. Valuable in revealing Brown's intellectual position at the end of his career as a novelist, it is poor in execution.

Clara Howard and *Jane Talbot,* we must conclude, are rather weak books that do not add much to Brown's reputation as a literary artist: they lack both the dramatic action and effective detail of his better work. In ruling out of his art such extraordinary elements as ventriloquism or sleepwalking, and such effective real events as the plague or Indian warfare, he abandoned the very devices which have made his books attractive to many readers. Though the modern taste may reject even these as motivating forces for character and action, they certainly function much more artistically in the novels where they occur than do the trite devices of distraught lovers, lost or forged letters, and convenient illnesses which take their place in Brown's last novels. In plotting, theme, and action, the earlier novels are vastly superior. The problems the characters face are made to seem real and pressing, and one can accept their attitudes and actions as credible in a way that he can never quite believe in a Clara Howard, a Mary Wilmot, or, perhaps, even a Jane Talbot. Of the two, *Jane Talbot* is intellectually the more interesting, and reveals, though weakly, something of Brown's artistic power. It, too, is essentially static, however, and falls far short of what one might expect from the author of *Wieland* and *Edgar Huntly.*

CHAPTE

IN CONCEI
Charles Bro
number of his
written while h
was published in
editor, but some
Life in 1815,[2] an
Fragment," was ev
Huntly.[3] Though a
to an understandin
literary talent, only
student today. "Thess
because of its theme:
a minor cause because
on Concealment; or, M
portance because, as Be
the complexity of Brown
method.[4] "A Lesson on C
group, but even it is of
in relation to the novels w

I

The same judgment can a
Brown did after the appeara
are two long quasi-historica
started earlier, but a major
tures, was very likely written
two pieces, "Sketches of a Hist
History of the Carrils and Orme
aginary history, but Brown treats
reporting facts. The time sequen
and episodes follow one another
between them—almost as if the sk

ments which happen
of the sketches reve
gious matters, much
though the tenor of
takes no stand for
maintains, rather,
As an odd kind o
Berthoff suggests,
years,[8] the works
of the fragments,
the careful attenti
The other writ
was largely non-
number of politi
1804 he complet
and Climate of
"Sketch of the
brother, who h
an edition of L
Of these wor
The first, publ
over the prosp
out that by a
France. The
take possessi
ber, 1802, a
of deposit
Western Am
goods, such
trade at wi
states. In A
the Cession
minent per
a French
a docume
and the a
sion. Wit
speaking
to remov
In the
Embass

[1

Claims to the Navigation of the Mississippi—Brown argues even more hotly for open war. Rather than send an emissary to Europe to negotiate the issue or to buy the territory, he writes, the United States should seize Louisiana at once and defend it against the French. Both of the pamphlets on Louisiana are effective political pieces which reveal a Brown quite different from the one who wrote the novels. Even the calmer pamphlets that Brown wrote several years later show a side of the novelist that should not be forgotten. *The British Treaty of Commerce and Navigation* (1807), which argues the superiority of the Jay Treaty of 1794 to that negotiated with Great Britain in 1806,[9] and *An Address to the Congress of the United States on the Utility and Justice of Restrictions upon Foreign Commerce* (1809), which takes a stand against the Embargo Act of 1807, are written in a kind of straightforward style seldom, if ever, apparent in his fiction. They certainly illustrate that Brown was quite at home in political controversy.

Much of Brown's work in these later years was editorial. In September, 1803, he began to publish the second of his journals, *The Literary Magazine and American Register*, which he continued to edit until 1807, when he abandoned the magazine in favor of *The American Register, or General Repository of History, Politics, and Science*. Five semi-annual volumes of this work appeared between November, 1807, and his death early in 1810. Both of these serials show Brown's shift of interest away from the purely literary; except for the *Memoirs of Carwin*, which appeared, somewhat irregularly, in the former between November, 1803, and March, 1805, Brown published little original fiction in *The Literary Magazine*.[10] By the time he took up *The American Register*, he had become absorbed in writing historical annals, and he published in this journal historical surveys of the periods covered by the volumes, digests of laws, and reports of books published both here and abroad. Indeed, at the time of his death, he had completed a large amount of work on yet another project, *A System of General Geography*, which further illustrates his turning away from the writing of fiction.[11]

Brown's last years were thus spent mostly in historical writing and editing; and, although this work should certainly not be dismissed as insignificant, it does represent a falling off from the truly important fiction he had already written. Yet Brown was probably not unhappy with the change. In the first issue of *The*

Literary Magazine in 1803, he made the astonishing statement that he would have more respect for himself if nothing he had written could be traced to him, and he included the enigmatic comment that he took "much blame" to himself for something which he had written.[12] Brown apparently did not regret abandoning fiction.

Despite his increasing illness, too, he seems to have been relatively happy. His marriage to Elizabeth Linn in 1804 and the birth of his four children—including twin sons and a daughter—brought him comfort and happiness. His health, however, always poor, began to fail; and, although he made several journeys in an attempt to regain it, he did not succeed. In November, 1809, he took to his bed and lingered for several months. He showed increasing signs of advanced tuberculosis and died, fully conscious until the end, most probably on February 21, 1810,[13] at the age of thirty-nine.

II A General Assessment

The life of Charles Brockden Brown was thus a short but unusually productive one. Even if one dismisses most of his minor fiction and editorial work as of relatively little significance to the general student today, his six completed novels and *Stephen Calvert* are still worthy of critical attention. Brown is not by any means a major writer, and readers of his fiction must be willing to accept serious faults in plotting, style, and characterization which they would not tolerate in more recent authors. Brown's books are admittedly defective; but, considering the time and the conditions under which they were written, they represent a truly important accomplishment. This is not to say that Brown's books must be valued because they are old, or because they represent the first significant achievement of an American novelist. Although such considerations undoubtedly play a part in any defense one might choose to make of his fiction, Brown's major novels deserve to be read not only for the interest they generate in their thematic development but also for the literary value which they certainly possess.

Any sound estimate of Brown's achievement must start with his themes, for his books are novels of ideas that impress one most strongly at first for the intellectuality which they clearly exhibit. This quality goes far beyond the simple exposition of radical doctrine that Clark sees in the books (192), or even the aphoristic power that Warfel observes in them.[14] Brown's examination of ideas in his fiction is much more fundamental than either of these views reveals; for, as Berthoff has correctly observed, the novels were themselves the testing grounds of ideas: vehicles not for the exposition but for the scrutiny of them.[15]

If one reads the books in these terms, he soon observes that Brown's treatment of contemporary ideas tends to proceed as if he were examining the relative strengths and weaknesses of opposite points of view. His characters, thus, are spread across the whole intellectual spectrum: they frequently represent one or another extreme of human behavior. One sees in them the influence of the rational and non-rational in human experience, of mind and feeling, of belief and unbelief, of benevolence and selfishness. All of his books, it seems fair to say, represent Brown's attempt to determine for himself the significance of each element in human behavior.

The most important question he raises, in view of his background and bent of mind, is the value of reason as a guide to life. That Brown firmly believed in the validity of human reason cannot be doubted, for even in books like *Wieland* and *Edgar Huntly*, which seem almost to represent the triumph of unreason, rationality is firmly in control once again at the end of the book. Many of the characters he presents as most attractive—like Clara Wieland or Constantia Dudley—are fundamentally rationalistic in their thinking; and, with the latter heroine, Brown clearly indicates his belief that a rational education for a young lady is absolutely necessary if she is to survive in the practical world. Departures from reason are always considered abnormalities in Brown's fiction, and his last novel, *Jane Talbot*, which may justly be taken to reflect his final intellectual position, clearly indicates his belief in the need for a rational basis for faith to protect the human being from the extremes of emotionalism. The point need not be dwelt upon. The whole direction of Brown's intellectual life and the development of his thought as it is revealed throughout his fiction clearly indicate the central position he would grant to human reason as a primary element in leading men to truth and guiding their actions.

This is not to say that Brown was, or remained for long, a naïve rationalist; for the evidence is conclusive that he saw some serious dangers in the paths of those who would attempt to lead the utterly rational life—and this point is underscored in a number of his books. Even his strongest rationalists sometimes get into trouble when they try to draw conclusions on the basis of sensory evidence with their minds alone. The influence of early impressions affects such characters as Clara and Theodore Wieland; the usual human passions lead Henry Pleyel astray. Even Constantia Dudley, who is obviously intended to represent the best and most rational of them all, nearly fails in the most important crisis of her life because, for all her rationality, she cannot hope to meet and overcome with her mind alone the insidious attacks on her virtue launched by the deceitful Ormond. All of these characters, it must be noted, have strong intellects; and all have been given what is supposed to be a superior education—yet all fail in meeting the challenge presented to their minds by what they see and hear in the external world. Their failure, then, one may conclude, clearly represents Brown's serious doubts that weak and fallible men can always arrive at truth simply through the use of their unaided minds.

An even more serious indictment of the rationalist view of the world is presented through the characters of Brown's intellectual villains, who represent the radical extreme to which the rationalist thinker may sometimes be led. Carwin, Ludloe, and Ormond are clearly identified with much of the radical thought we know Brown became acquainted with in his early reading, and all are engaged to some degree with plans to remake the world and men according to rationalist principles. Significantly, all three are clearly villains. Ludloe persecutes Carwin, who himself takes pleasure in dominating the lives of others, and Ormond ruins the life of Helena Cleves and would do the same to Constantia Dudley were he not thwarted before he can accomplish his purpose. Since Brown consistently makes the characters both radical thinkers and obvious villains, it seems certain that he intended the reader to question the value of their principles and to perceive the need for some restraint to be placed upon their soaring thoughts and vaunting ambitions.[16] Their minds alone are not sufficient to serve such a purpose, for Carwin and Ormond both reveal themselves capable of self-deception and rationalization.

Other characters, too, by no means so villainous as these, reveal Brown's apparent belief in the ease with which the mind of man may deceive itself. The best example, no doubt, is the character of Arthur Mervyn, who starts his career as if he were merely a naïve boy at the mercy of evil forces loose in the world but who eventually shows himself to be the master of his environment. The self-deception that Mervyn, perhaps unconsciously, practices is different, however, from that in Carwin or Ormond. Unconcerned with power or dominance over others, Mervyn converts his selfishness into the appearance of benevolence; and, by seeming to act on only the best of motives, he succeeds in gaining just what he wants from others. Mervyn maintains the mask of benevolence throughout his career, and insists to the end that his motives are unquestionably pure. The reader, however, can see behind the overt actions of the man to the true motivation that lies behind his deeds, and thus perceive the deceptions of which men are capable.

A similar view is surely presented through the actions of Edgar Huntly, who possesses a number of the qualities already considered. Like Brown's intellectual villains, he has been led into erroneous opinions through the arguments of Waldegrave; like Clara and Theodore Wieland, he is influenced to some extent by the past: his parents' deaths at the hands of the Indians. Like them, too, he attempts to arrive at a just interpretation of what he perceives in the world through his senses, but his inferences, like theirs, are frequently shown to be in error. He shares the false benevolence of Arthur Mervyn, and he sometimes reveals himself to be as compulsive in his actions. Indeed, Huntly would seem to present a most telling attack on the validity of human reasoning were he not also, like Clara Wieland, eventually reclaimed at the end of the book. At any rate, it seems perfectly clear in view of all this evidence that Brown was no naïve rationalist by the time he wrote his novels. Reason is still of great value in all of these books and represents the standard in terms of which the aberrations of the characters may be judged. Since all of these characters, however, fall such easy prey to the deceptions of themselves and others, one may surely conclude that Brown placed no blind faith in human reason.

Brown was even more critical of the emotional approach to life; for the characters he drew who follow this path are shown to be even less successful than those who try to guide their lives by reason alone. The highly volatile Stephen Calvert is a case in point, as are the main female characters in his last two novels. Clara Howard deceives herself into believing that she is acting on rational principles; but she, like Jane Talbot, is largely a creature of emotion. All of these characters are straws blown by the wind. With no fixed principles or rational guides to action, each is the prey of any emotion he feels and is easily swayed by the influence of others. Stephen Calvert vacillates between his cousin Louisa and Clelia Neville; Jane Talbot is influenced in turn by Mrs. Fielder and Henry Colden. Jane, moreover, falls victim to the emotional appeals of her brother; and Clara Howard gives up her supposedly firm resolves when she hears of Philip's illness and fears that he may die. There can be no question that Brown completely dismisses the emotions as proper guides to conduct.

Brown does not let the matter end here. Indeed, one might argue, he could hardly afford to do so without giving the world over entirely to the non-rational elements in man. Convinced of the value of human reason, he had of necessity to come to grips with the problem of the many non-rational influences exerted upon the individual man and to affirm some standard by which the characters might be kept from falling into error. In *Wieland,* this function is provided, in part at least, by Clara's uncle, a doctor, who tries to help her back to sanity and who at one time explains scientifically the mania that afflicts her brother. The point of view which the uncle represents, however, plays no really important part in Brown's subsequent fiction. Rather, Brown seems to affirm yet another element as necessary in one's intellectual make-up if he is to avoid the errors into which both his mind and his passions can lead him. That element is religion, clearly presented in *Ormond* as the one element needed by Constantia Dudley to enable her to withstand successfully the evil machinations of her would-be seducer.

Religion is a subject seldom considered of much importance in discussions of Brown,[17] but the vital role it plays in the intellectual drama of *Ormond* justifies a recognition of its influence when it occupies a less obvious place in other of Brown's books. Thus, once the reader is aware that the absence of religion is to be seen as a serious flaw in Constantia's education, he may certainly consider a similar omission in the training of Clara and Theodore Wieland as equally significant; for the implication is strong that part of the trouble which brother and sister experience may derive from this lack. Indeed, there is even a hint in *Edgar Huntly* that the protagonist of that book is acting under the influence of the irreligious principles that Waldegrave had instilled in him and which Huntly has not entirely given up by the time of the action. Such evidence is by no means strong and might not perhaps be at all convincing did not Brown's final novel, *Jane Talbot*, make abundantly clear his affirmation of the need for religious faith if one is to lead a satisfactory life. It is doubly significant, perhaps, that in this book it is a Godwinian rationalist who is at last converted to religious belief.

Other evidence clearly indicates that Brown turned increasingly to an affirmation of religion as he grew older—so much so that one is tempted to see the depiction of Henry Colden's intellectual development as fundamentally autobiographical.[18] Be that as it may, it is clear that by 1803, Brown openly supported religious values; for, in "The Editors' Address to the Public" in the first issue of *The Literary Magazine*, he expressed his awareness of the bold attacks that had been made on "the foundations of religion and morality" in his times. It was important, he went on to say, that in presenting a magazine to the public, he should explicitly state his policy. "Without equivocation or reserve," he announced himself to be "the ardent friend and the willing champion of the Christian religion," who sought as the reward of his labors the consciousness that he had "in some degree however inconsiderable, contributed to recommend the practice of religious duties."[19] One cannot, of course, apply a passage like this to the books he had written some three to five years earlier; but the statement is significant in revealing the intellectual position toward which he had probably been moving during his writing career.[20]

Because he is concerned with questions of religion in *Wieland*, it seems fair to conclude that by the time he wrote that novel—and certainly as early as *Ormond*—Brown had begun to consider the value of religious faith in the properly regulated life. In none of his fiction is Brown very specific on what that faith should be, though it is clear, of course, that it ought not to be the type professed by the two Wielands, father and son. It is obvious, too, that he placed no trust in purely emotional religious feelings, for Jane Talbot's early piety is dismissed as unsubstantial; and he certainly believed that religious faith should have a firm rational basis, for he illustrates in the eventual union of Henry Colden and Jane Talbot the acceptance of both reason and faith which he finally presents as necessary for a successful life. Brown himself, was neither a philosopher nor a theologian but a literary artist; and, if he leaves his statement of belief rather vague, that is only to be expected of a man in his time and place, and with his intellectual background. In raising the questions he does in his books, however, he sounds a note that was to re-echo, in one way or another, in a considerable amount of subsequent American fiction.

James Fenimore Cooper comes immediately to mind. He too, especially in his later novels, became increasingly concerned with questions of reason and faith; and in one novel, *The Sea Lions,* he presents an action which strongly resembles the end of *Jane Talbot.* Though Cooper may be more specific in expressing his religious views, the basic question is fundamentally the same in both works; the differences merely reflect the personal beliefs of the two men. Much the same conclusion can be drawn from the obvious similarities in theme between Brown's works and those of two other successors, Nathaniel Hawthorne and Herman Melville. The rival claims of head and heart, of reason and emotion, are important concerns of all three, so that Brown may surely be called a forerunner of both men in the development of the concept. Other thematic relations between Brown and subsequent writers can, no doubt, be made; and, though one would not wish by any means to suggest that Brown's importance as a writer can be completely defined by such relations, a perception of them is surely necessary if one is to understand his position in American literature in its full significance.

More important are Brown's claims to attention as a literary artist; for it is, after all, as a novelist and not as a thinker that he must be remembered. His place as a writer of fiction has always been difficult to determine; and, because of the faults in his books, it will always be open to question. His novels are all structurally weak. The best of them, it must be admitted, are among the most seriously flawed; *Wieland, Edgar Huntly,* and *Arthur Mervyn* fall far short of being clearly organized and well-integrated books. Indeed, only *Jane Talbot* and *Ormond,* much poorer novels, approach the structural unity the twentieth-century critic demands in fiction. Among his weaknesses, too, must be added the defective style, with its inappropriate words and involved circumlocutions; the thinness of his descriptions of the physical setting; and the lack of dimension in some of his characters. With such serious flaws as these, one might ask, how can his novels survive? For they seem to be weak in all of those elements which are generally considered to be essential ones in all good fiction.

The answer is simply that in each of these areas, Brown displays qualities that more than make up for his faults. Though each of his better novels, taken as a whole, is structurally flawed, each also contains long and important stretches in which the action moves forward with a pace and an interest that completely absorb the reader. The handling of the subplot in *Wieland* is indefensible, yet the reader quickly forgets it once he becomes involved in the problems of Clara Wieland and in the suspenseful main events of the story, which move with an inexorable sweep toward the dénouement. The same is true of *Edgar Huntly*. Clithero's account of his past and Weymouth's digression are, strictly speaking, discordant notes in the basic tone of the book, yet the compelling episodes of Huntly's thrilling and significant frontier adventures carry the novel forward to a strong and meaningful conclusion. In like manner, the chaotic second part of *Arthur Mervyn* cannot entirely detract from the rather well-rounded and fascinating story which Brown tells in the first. In each of these books, major parts of the action reveal an artistic talent in the author that is not as apparent in the novel as a whole. So important are the major episodes, however, that the books can be read and enjoyed for the artistic value of those dominant, well-presented parts.

A similar judgment can be made on Brown's style. Though it is not at all difficult to find in his books examples of his writing that are clearly ludicrous, such defects are not really so serious as they seem to be when the sentences are pulled out of context and viewed in isolation. Brown is, of course, no great stylist; but, in his three best books, the style serves as a suitable vehicle for the action presented. One can believe in Clara Wieland's distraught language, overdone though it may sometimes be, for it fits her character and predicament. One perceives the irony apparent in Mervyn's account of his life and accepts the portrayal of Huntly's compulsive actions because the language in which the characters analyze their motives and recount their deeds is, for all its faults, fundamentally convincing. The descriptions, too, weak though they certainly are in the broader aspects of setting, serve an important thematic function in both *Arthur Mervyn* and *Edgar Huntly*, and manage to hold the reader in many specific episodes, like Clara Wieland's confrontation of the danger in her closet, Arthur Mervyn's experiences during the plague in Philadelphia, or Edgar Huntly's adventures near the elm tree or deep in the cave. These scenes have a reality and an immediacy that can only be attributed to Brown's skill in handling the language.

In characterization, too, Brown shows considerable artistic talent. One does not really know what his characters look like, and even some of the major ones are certainly weak. Yet faults like these are more than overbalanced by the psychological validity that his best characters undoubtedly possess. The descent into madness that Clara Wieland and Edgar Huntly make is convincingly depicted; and, although one may know little about their external appearance, the central reason for their existence in the story—the psychological aberration—is presented so well through their self-revelation that the character as a whole takes life from it. Arthur Mervyn, too, possesses a psychological reality that is unforgettable; Wieland, in his speech to the court, is a believable maniac; and lesser characters than these, like Carwin or Helena Cleves, have an individual quality about them which prevents their becoming only flat representations of intellectual or emotional states. Even Constantia Dudley, despite her collapse as a character at the end of *Ormond,* shows a feminine charm which makes her a believable person.

Taken on balance, the novels of Charles Brockden Brown are by no means so poor as a simple enumeration of their faults might seem to indicate. Overriding the major flaws are strong virtues which clearly reveal the undeniable genius of the author. He could tell an absorbing, suspenseful story through the actions of psychologically believable characters; and, at the same time, he could make the physical movement of the plot the vehicle for an intellectual drama which has an interest of its own. At the levels of both action and theme, the novels generate an intellectual and emotional power that raises them above the level of mere forerunners of later and better fiction. Their historical significance, of course, is unquestioned; but it must not be overemphasized. In his brief career as a novelist, Charles Brockden Brown did indeed initiate a kind of fiction that was to become an important type in subsequent American literature. At the same time, he created in the best parts of his better novels— *Wieland, Edgar Huntly,* and *Arthur Mervyn*— a body of work which can still be read with considerable pleasure today.

Notes and References

Quotations from Brown's novels are from the edition published in six volumes by the Kennikat Press (Port Washington, N. Y., 1963), an exact reproduction of the edition of 1887. Page references to the various novels in my text are to volume and page numbers in this edition. The full reference to secondary sources is given only once below. Thereafter, whenever a biographer or critic is named in the text, a page reference indicates that his work has already been cited. For Dunlap, Warfel, and Clark, page references are to their biographies of Brown; other works by them are specified by title in the footnotes.

Chapter One

1. For the poem, see Harry R. Warfel, *Charles Brockden Brown: American Gothic Novelist* (Gainesville, Fla., 1949), pp. 32-33; for the essays, entitled "The Rhapsodist," see Charles Brockden Brown, *The Rhapsodist and Other Uncollected Writings*, ed. by Harry R. Warfel (New York, 1943), pp. 1-24.

2. Richard Chase, *The American Novel and Its Tradition* (Garden City, N. Y., 1957), p. 37.

3. R. W. B. Lewis, *The American Adam: Innocence, Tragedy, and Tradition in the Nineteenth Century* (Chicago, 1955), p. 92.

4. See the references to Brown and his novels in the following: *The Letters of John Keats*, ed. by Hyder E. Rollins (Cambridge, Mass., 1958), II, 173; (for Shelley) Thomas Love Peacock, *Works*, ed. by Henry Cole (London, 1875), III, 409-10; Edgar Allan Poe, *Works*, ed. by James A. Harrison (New York, 1902), XI, 206, XII, 224, 249, XVI, 41; William Hickling Prescott, "Memoir of Charles Brockden Brown, the American Novelist," *Biographical and Critical Miscellanies* (Philadelphia, 1865), pp. 1-56; Nathaniel Hawthorne, *Works* (Boston, 1882), II, 198; John Greenleaf Whittier, *Writings* (Boston, 1895), VII, 392-95; Margaret Fuller, *Writings*, ed. by Mason Wade (New York, 1941), pp. 374, 377-80.

5. George Snell, *The Shapers of American Fiction, 1798-1947* (New York, 1947), pp. 39, 44.

6. Leslie A. Fiedler, *Love and Death in the American Novel* (New York, 1960), p. 143.

7. Martin S. Vilas, *Charles Brockden Brown: A Study of Early American Fiction* (Burlington, Vt., 1904), p. 27.

8. David Lee Clark, *Charles Brockden Brown: Pioneer Voice of America* (Durham, N. C., 1952), p. 192.

9. Alexander Cowie, *The Rise of the American Novel* (New York, 1951), p. 91.

10. Larzer Ziff, "A Reading of *Wieland*," *PMLA*, LXXVII (1962), 55, footnote 3.

11. Warfel, p. 9; Lewis, pp. 95-96. Both cite passages from *Arthur Mervyn* in support of their opinions.

12. Warfel, p. 36; Clark states, however, that Brown left Wilcocks' office "during the summer of 1793" (37).

13. Warfel, pp. 7, 26-27.

14. Warfel, pp. 7, 27; Clark, pp. 110, 113.

15. Warfel, p. 17.

16. For a discussion of the New York Friendly Club and Brown's relation to it, see James E. Cronin, "Elihu Hubbard Smith and the New York Friendly Club, 1795-1798," *PMLA*, LXIV (1949), 471-79.

17. Clark, however, argues that it may have been written as early as the fall of 1796 (116-17).

18. Warfel, p. 82. It should be noted, however, that Smith was reluctant to print these parts not because he was opposed to the ideas, but because he did not think it expedient to publish them.

19. William Dunlap, *The Life of Charles Brockden Brown: together with Selections from the Rarest of His Printed Works, from His Original Letters, and from His Manuscripts Before Unpublished* (Philadelphia, 1815), I, 70.

20. *Ibid.*, I, 57, 169.

21. *Ibid.*, I, 91.

22. A very different view from that expressed here is Ernest Marchand's suggestion that Brown may have put radical opinions into the mouths of his villains so that he could place them before his readers "without bearing the onus of holding them himself." This opinion strikes me as hardly defensible since such a practice would violate all sound principles of both art and propaganda. See Ernest Marchand, "Introduction," *Ormond*, by Charles Brockden Brown (New York, 1937), p. xxix.

23. Dunlap, I, 51.

24. *Ibid.*, I, 51, 53. For Wilkins' reaction to Brown's melancholy and other expressions of self-condemnation by Brown, see David Lee Clark, "Unpublished Letters of Charles Brockden Brown and W. W. Wilkins," *University of Texas Studies in English*, XXVII (1948), 84, 102, 103.

25. Warfel, pp. 56-64.

26. *Ibid.*, pp. 86-88.

27. He began a "Philadelphia novel" in the fall of 1795—possibly an early draft of *Arthur Mervyn*—and he clearly had *Caleb Williams* in mind at the time. See Warfel, pp. 54-55.

28. See Brown's letter to his brother James, dated February 15, 1799, quoted in Dunlap, II, 98. Another résumé of the plot of *Arthur Mervyn*, thinly disguised with different names, but with little emphasis on the second part, appears in "Walstein's School of History," published in two issues of *The Monthly Magazine and American Review*, August and September-December, 1799, and reprinted in Warfel's edition of *The Rhapsodist*, pp. 145-56, esp. 154-56.

29. For additional evidence that Brown may have changed and developed his themes as he wrote, see Ziff's analysis of *Wieland*, esp. pp. 53-54.

30. W. B. Berthoff, " 'A Lesson on Concealment': Brockden Brown's Method in Fiction," *Philological Quarterly*, XXXVII (1958), 45-57, esp. 46-48.

31. Although part was apparently set in type, the novel was never published, owing to the sudden death of the publisher and the recalcitrance of his executors. See Warfel, p. 91. An "Advertisement" for the book and an "Extract" from it were published in *The Weekly Magazine* in March, 1798, and are reprinted in Warfel's edition of *The Rhapsodist*, pp. 135-41.

32. Cf., for example, Numbers IV and V of "The Man at Home" (*The Rhapsodist*, ed. by Warfel, pp. 47-56), and Chapter VII of *Ormond* (VI, 61-68).

Chapter Two

1. In addition to those mentioned in Chapter 1, footnote 1 above, these include the following pieces, which appeared in the Philadelphia *Weekly Magazine*: the opening chapters of *Arthur Mervyn*, published from June 16 to August 25, 1798; "The Man at Home," February 3 to April 28, 1798; "A Series of Original Letters," April 21 to June 2, 1798; and the "Advertisement" of and an "Extract" from *Sky-Walk*, March 17 and March 24, 1798.

2. Warfel, p. 100. Cf. Jacob Blanck, *Bibliography of American Literature* (New Haven, 1955), I, 302. Warfel corrects the dating error on p. 110 of his biography on September 14, 1798. See Harry R. Warfel, *Footnotes to Charles Brockden Brown: American Gothic Novelist (1949)* (Gainesville, Fla., 1953), p. 7.

3. Warfel, pp. 110-11. The reviews, according to Warfel, appeared in the New York *Spectator*, November 10, 1798, and January 2, 1799. Warfel also mentions a third in *The American Review and Literary Journal*, July-September, 1801.

4. Fred Lewis Pattee, "Introduction," *Wieland; or, The Transformation, together with Memoirs of Carwin, the Biloquist, a Fragment*, by Charles Brockden Brown (New York, 1926), pp. xxv-xli.

5. Cf. William M. Manly, "The Importance of Point of View in Brockden Brown's *Wieland*," *American Literature*, XXXV (1963), 309-21. Manly's article, which appeared after this chapter was written, covers some of the same points treated here.

6. This point has been clearly established by Warfel, p. 107, and by Ziff, pp. 53-54. Indeed, Warfel had observed as early as 1940 that *Wieland* is based upon this psychology, citing as a specific source a German novel, Cajetan Tschink's *Geisterseher*, translated as *The Victim of Magical Delusion* (1795), which also makes use of the psychology. Indeed, Warfel cites a long passage from the introduction to the translation which may have influenced Brown's depiction of Wieland as a man who seeks direct communication with God. See Harry R. Warfel, "Charles Brockden Brown's German Sources," *Modern Language Quarterly*, I (1940), 361-65.

7. It must be noted, however, that neither Theodore nor Clara Wieland carries this belief to a rationalistic extreme; for, in the course of the novel, both accept the possibility of direct communication from the Deity. Nonetheless, as shall be seen below, much of their thought and action reveals their general acceptance of the psychology of the times.

8. Cf. Ziff, pp. 53-54.

9. See Chapter 1 above.

10. Although it is generally assumed that Brown follows Mrs. Radcliffe in

giving a natural explanation of the phenomena he uses, it should be noted that he leaves elements of the occurrence unexplained—the blow on the arm, for example—and he hints that the father's account of the incident did not reveal everything that happened. His footnote, however, does cite contemporary sources for the incident. See also Clark, p. 167.

11. Brown clearly underscores the "strong passions" of Pleyel (I, 138) not only in this passage but also earlier in the book when Clara mentions the "torments of jealousy" Pleyel undergoes when he fails to get an expected letter from his fiancée in Europe (I, 60).

12. Wieland, however, did say shortly before this speech that he is a judge "who is willing to question his own senses when they plead against" her (I, 128).

13. Cf. Ziff, p. 53.

14. Cf. Ziff, who maintains that the conclusion of the book contradicts the main action by affirming once more at the end the principles of contemporary psychology (53-54).

15. Memoirs of Carwin, the Biloquist, printed in Dunlap, II, 200-63, esp. 229-31.

16. See, for example, ibid., pp. 226-27, 238-39.

17. Although neither Wieland nor the Memoirs fragment makes entirely clear what happened between Carwin and Ludloe, we do know from Wieland that Carwin has been accused, falsely it would seem, of robbery and murder and is hiding in America to escape Ludloe's persecution (I, 148-49, 218, 258).

18. Warfel, pp. 104-5; Clark, p. 169.

19. Cf. Ziff, who maintains that it is easier to explain Wieland's delusion in terms of his lack of religious training, than of any "prejudiced expectations" (54). See, too, his comment that the Wielands' lack of formal education insulated them from sectarian doctrine because the colleges and schools of the time were all religious ones (55).

20. See, for example, Pattee, pp. xli-xlii; Warfel, p. 108.

21. Cf., for example, the first few paragraphs of each novel.

22. Brown's use of the multiple point of view in Wieland has been noted by Pattee, p. xlii; Warfel, pp. 105-6; and Cowie, p. 49. Cf. Manly, pp. 320-21. In addition, Berthoff has observed its recurring use in Brown's fiction. See " 'A Lesson on Concealment,' " p. 49, footnote 5.

Chapter Three

1. "Diary of William Dunlap," Collections of the New York Historical Society, LXII-LXIV (New York, 1930), pp. 338-39. The three volumes are paged continuously throughout.

2. See Chapter 2, footnote 1 above.

3. "Diary of William Dunlap," p. 342. The dates of Brown's arrival in and departure from Perth Amboy mentioned in this paragraph are from the same source, pp. 342, 346.

4. Dunlap, II, 93.

5. Warfel, p. 128.

6. Cf. Marchand, pp. xxix-xxx.

7. It should be observed, too, that until he meets Constantia, Ormond has a very low opinion of the capabilities of women, a view which runs counter to the whole theme of *Alcuin*. See, for example, VI, 118-19, 148.

8. Dunlap was the first to perceive Brown's use of the Illuminati in *Memoirs of Carwin*. See "Diary of William Dunlap," p. 339. More recent discussions are Lillie D. Loshe, *The Early American Novel* (New York, 1907), pp. 41-43; and Clark, pp. 174, 188-90.

9. Cf. Prescott, who links Constantia Dudley with Griselda in Chaucer and Boccaccio (p. 26).

10. Cf. Loshe, p. 46; Marchand, pp. xxxii-xxxiv.

11. VI, 113. An incident in which Ormond uses his talent to gain information appears in VI, 130-33.

12. It should be noted, too, that Ormond also uses physical means to influence Constantia, for he helps the Dudley family escape from poverty, and he is instrumental in restoring Dudley his sight (VI, 271-72).

13. Warfel, p. 131. He also notes the significance of Constantia's name.

14. From this incident as well as from Ormond's great talent for disguise, the novel derives its subtitle, *The Secret Witness*. See especially VI, 252-53.

15. This house had once been owned by Stephen Dudley, acquired by Ormond, given to Helena Cleves, and willed to Constantia (VI, 257-58).

16. Marchand, p. xxxii; Warfel, pp. 130, 132-33. A dissenting view may be found in Clark, p. 173.

17. See the defense of the change in Ormond's behavior quoted in Dunlap, II, 15-16.

18. Cf. Marchand, who believes that the Craig episode receives too much emphasis and that both the Baxter story and the early history of Sophia are digressive (p. xxxvi).

19. See VI, 51, 56, 39-40.

20. Comments on the style of the novel may be found in Marchand, pp. xxxvi-xxxvii; Warfel, p. 137.

Chapter Four

1. Dunlap, II, 93.

2. *Ibid.*, II, 98.

3. Blanck cites evidence which indicates that it was published on March 7/8, 1799 (I, 302). Cf. Warfel, who also cites evidence to show that the day of publication was May 21, 1799 (243).

4. Dunlap, II, 97-98.

5. According to Warfel, the book was printed by July 4, 1800 (145), and his *Footnotes* cite the *Universal Gazette* for that date as his source (8). Blanck, however, cites advertisements in New York newspapers announcing the date of publication as September 3, 1800 (I, 304).

6. See W. B. Berthoff, "Adventures of the Young Man: An Approach to Charles Brockden Brown," *American Quarterly*, IX (1957), 421-34, and "Introduction," *Arthur Mervyn*, by Charles Brockden Brown (New York, 1962), where Berthoff considers elements from both parts of the novel in his interpretation of its meaning.

7. See Clark, p. 181; Lewis, pp. 94, 98. Indeed, in his discussion of the novel, Clark devotes much of his space to a comparison of *Arthur Mervyn* with Godwin's *Caleb Williams,* which in some respects it strongly resembles. See pp. 178-79.

8. See Warfel, pp. 146-47; Clark, p. 181.

9. See, for example, Vilas, p. 33; Clark, p. 179. Cowie also stresses the realism, but sees a humanitarian motive behind the descriptions (81).

10. Berthoff, "Adventures of the Young Man," pp. 426-28.

11. This concept is the whole point of Berthoff's article, but see especially p. 425. See also Lewis, pp. 97-98.

12. Berthoff, "Adventures of the Young Man," p. 426; "Introduction," p. xvi.

13. Mervyn comes from a family of children almost all of whom have died "as they attained the age of nineteen or twenty" (One sister, we later learn, committed suicide after being seduced). He believes, therefore, that he may reasonably anticipate "the same premature fate" (II, 17), a belief which Berthoff sees as the motivating factor in Mervyn's eager grasping for life. See "Adventures of the Young Man," p. 430. Mervyn does not succumb to this fate, but his belief renders plausible his later return to Philadelphia during the plague.

14. Wallace, it should be noted, turns out to be the same young man who gulled him on his first night in the city (II, 166, 175).

15. Dunlap, II, 97-98. Cf. Lewis, p. 98, who reads the second part in these terms.

16. Cf. Berthoff, "Introduction," p. xvi.

17. See especially *ibid.,* p. xvii.

18. The shift of Mervyn's affection from Eliza Hadwin to Achsa Fielding has several times been commented on by readers. Dunlap felt that Eliza was abandoned "in a manner as unexpected as disgusting" (II, 40); and Peacock reports that Shelley was displeased with the shift and concluded from it that Brown wanted to bring his book "to an uncomfortable conclusion" (*Works,* III, 409). See also Berthoff, "Adventures of the Young Man," p. 432.

19. That Mervyn himself is psychologically uneasy with his successful marriage is perhaps revealed near the end of the book by a fit of sleepwalking and by the dream he has in which he is stabbed in the breast by the dead Mr. Fielding! Mervyn, however, does not allow such thoughts or actions to disturb him for long. See Berthoff, "Adventures of the Young Man," p. 432.

20. Berthoff, "Introduction," p. xvii.

21. *Ibid.,* p. xvii.

22. *Ibid.,* p. xviii.

23. Indeed, if, as Warfel suggests, the "Philadelphia novel" Brown was working on in 1795 was an early version of *Arthur Mervyn* (54), the novel may have been written over a five year period. In any event, it is likely that he was at work on it for perhaps two years, 1798-1800.

24. Cf. Berthoff, "Adventures of the Young Man," p. 433.

25. Cf. Berthoff, "Introduction," p. xviii.

26. Cf. Lewis, p. 96.

Chapter Five

1. Warfel, p. 154. Blanck records that the novel was advertised in a Philadelphia newspaper, July 30-August 15, 1799. Volume One of *Edgar Huntly* was announced as "In the Press" and to be "Published in a few Days" (I, 304). Cf. Clark, p. 174.

2. Berthoff, "Adventures of the Young Man," p. 422. See also Fiedler, p. 144.

3. Warfel, p. 155. Although Clark cites an earlier treatment of the Indian in fiction, he believes that Brown demonstrated the value of the material (176).

4. John Neal, *American Writers: A Series of Papers Contributed to Blackwood's Magazine (1824-1825)*, ed. by Fred Lewis Pattee (Durham, N. C., 1937), p. 68. Cf. Lulu Rumsey Wiley, *The Sources and Influence of the Novels of Charles Brockden Brown* (New York, 1950), pp. 215-17; Warfel, p. 155; Cowie, p. 85; Chase, p. 36; Fiedler, p. 140. The edition of *The Spy* containing the Preface cited here is that of 1821.

5. Cf. Albert Keiser, *The Indian in American Literature* (New York, 1933), pp. 33-37; Warfel, p. 156.

6. See the Preface to *Edgar Huntly* (IV, 3-4).

7. Brown had, however, created two characters who had withdrawn to the wilderness: the Rhapsodist, who lived on the banks of the Ohio (*The Rhapsodist*, ed. by Warfel, pp. 13-15), and Stephen Calvert, who moved to the shores of Lake Michigan to avoid the "temptation and calamity" of society (Dunlap, II, 274-75). In neither case does Brown make much use of the material. It should be noted here, too, that since this chapter was written an article has appeared that covers some of the material treated in this and subsequent paragraphs. See Kenneth Bernard, "Charles Brockden Brown and the Sublime," *The Personalist*, XLV (1964), 235-49.

8. In addition to the biographers cited above, see especially Chase, p. 36.

9. Warfel, p. 160.

10. Cf. Fiedler, who sees "the cave as a metaphor for the mysteries of the human heart" (147).

11. Cf. Warfel, who also notes the parallel between the two characters (160).

12. It should be noted in passing that, as Warfel observes, the Weymouth-Waldegrave relationship parallels in one respect the Mrs. Lorimer-Wiatte one, in that Weymouth, like Mrs. Lorimer, believes that his life is inseparably tied up with that of another, in his case, Waldegrave (161).

13. Cf. Fiedler, p. 143.

14. Cf. Cowie, p. 84.

15. This is, of course, the second symbolic death that Huntly undergoes.

16. This is Huntly's third symbolic death, for those who shoot at him are certain that he has perished in the water.

17. Cf. Warfel, who believes that Huntly's madness is the same as that of the two Wielands (160).

18. Cf. Snell, who finds the framework of *Edgar Huntly* "entirely incredible" (44); and Fiedler, who defends the improbabilities of the book on psychological grounds (144).

19. That the cave scene is a possible source for Poe's story has been argued in David Lee Clark, "The Sources of Poe's 'The Pit and the Pendulum,'" *Modern Language Notes*, XLIV, (1929), 349-56.

20. Cf. Cowie, who also believes that Brown's work in the frontier scenes need not "be accounted any less successful than Poe's" (84).

21. Cf. Warfel, p. 159.

Chapter Six

1. According to Blanck, *Clara Howard* was announced as *"this day published"* in a Philadelphia newspaper advertisement dated June 22, 1801. *Jane Talbot* was announced as *"in the press"* by a Philadelphia journal, August 21, 1801, and as *"just received"* in a Baltimore newspaper, December 19, 1801 (I, 305). Warfel, however, lists the date of *Clara Howard* as July 2, 1801 (191, 243), and that of *Jane Talbot* as simply late in the same year (197).

2. It was published in Great Britain, however, as the major part of *Carwin, the Biloquist, and Other American Tales and Pieces* (London, 1822).

3. II, 274-472. Citations in both text and footnotes throughout the discussion of *Stephen Calvert* are to volume and page numbers in Dunlap.

4. Berthoff, "Adventures of the Young Man," p. 422.

5. See especially the scene in which Sidney encounters the real Felix and mistakes him for his twin (II, 467-70).

6. Felix and Stephen are shown to have different colored hair and eyes, and Stephen has a scar which puzzles Clelia at one point because she does not remember having noticed it before (II, 410-12, 470).

7. Cf. Berthoff, "Adventures of the Young Man," pp. 424-25.

8. Cf. *Ibid.*, p. 422.

9. For a brief discussion of Brown's possible relations with this journal, see Warfel, pp. 188-89.

10. Warfel, *Footnotes*, p. 10. Warfel cites a reference which indicates that the date on p. 189 of his biography should read "late in 1800."

11. Dunlap, II, 100.

12. VI, 291, 304, 347.

13. Cf. Warfel, p. 192; Loshe, p. 46. Both see Clara as similar to Constantia.

14. Cf. Clark, p. 182; Loshe, pp. 47-48. Both compare Philip's experience with Mervyn's strange romance with Achsa Fielding. Neither, however, considers the women's wealth as a possible motive for the young men's actions. See also Wiley, pp. 175-76.

15. In this connection, one must not place too much weight on the subtitle of the book, for the edition of 1801 appeared as *Clara Howard; In a Series of Letters*, with a hero named Edward Harley. The hero's name was changed to Philip Stanley and the book was called *Philip Stanley; or, The Enthusiasm of Love* in the London edition of 1807. American editions of the book since that of 1827 bear the title *Clara Howard; or, The Enthusiasm of Love*, and the hero's name remains Philip Stanley. See Warfel, p. 191.

16. Cf. Warfel, pp. 199-200.

17. Cf. *ibid.*, pp. 198-99.

18. A statement of the importance of the concept in both Hawthorne and Melville may be found in F. O. Matthiessen, *American Renaissance: Art and Expression in the Age of Emerson and Whitman* (New York, 1941), p. 345.

Chapter Seven

1. Minor works in *The Monthly Magazine* written by Brown or attributed to him include: "Thessalonica: A Roman Story" (May, 1799), "Portrait of an Emigrant" (June, 1799), "A Lesson on Concealment; or, Memoirs of Mary Selwyn" (March, 1800), "The Trials of Arden" (July, 1800), "Friendship: An Original Letter" (July, 1800), "The Household: A Fragment" (August, 1800), "Original Letters" (August, 1800). Cf. Carl Van Doren, "Minor Tales of Brockden Brown, 1798-1800," *The Nation*, C (1915), 46-47; Warfel, pp. 175-76; Clark, pp. 133-34. Van Doren points out, moreover, that "Original Letters" are part of the same story as the "Jessica" fragment, printed in Dunlap. See also footnote 2 below.

2. These are "Jessica," I, 108-69; "Dialogues" (on music and painting), II, 122-39; "Signior Adini," II, 140-69; "The Scribbler," II, 264-73. The first and third are unnamed in Dunlap. "Thessalonica" is also reprinted here (II, 170-99), and "Friendship" appears as part of "Jessica" (I, 120-24).

3. This story—a narrative of Cicero's death told by a faithful retainer—comprises a separately numbered forty-eight pages at the end of Volume III in the second edition, 1799. See Blanck, I, 304.

4. Berthoff, "'A Lesson on Concealment,'" pp. 47-48, 55-57.

5. W. B. Berthoff, "Charles Brockden Brown's Historical 'Sketches': A Consideration," *American Literature*, XXVIII (1956), 149. For much of the interpretation which follows in this paragraph, I am indebted to Berthoff's article, esp. pp. 150-54.

6. These may be found in Dunlap, I, 170-258, 262-396.

7. Cf. Warfel, pp. 71-72.

8. Berthoff, "Charles Brockden Brown's Historical 'Sketches,'" pp. 150, 153-54.

9. Clark, it should be noted, argues that this pamphlet is not by Brown (261), although it is ascribed to him by Dunlap (II, 69-74).

10. Warfel mentions only the *Memoirs of Carwin* (222). Alfred Weber ascribes to Brown the short story "Somnambulism: A Fragment," which appeared in the issue for May, 1805. See Alfred Weber, "Eine neu entdeckte Kurzgeschichte C. B. Browns," *Jahrbuch für Amerikastudien*, VIII (1963), 280-96. Clark ascribes to Brown the five part story "Omar and Fatima; or, The Apothecary of Ispahan," which appeared between July and December, 1807. See Clark, p. 228.

11. Of this work, only the prospectus has survived; the manuscript was lost after Brown's death. See Warfel, p. 234.

12. "The Editors' Address to the Public," *The Literary Magazine and American Register*, I (1803), 4. The principal reason for this opinion, he goes on to say, is that while time enlarges and refines a man's powers, the world judges his mature "capacities and principles" from what he wrote as a youth (5).

13. Warfel, *Footnotes*, p. 12. Although most accounts of Brown's life give February 22 as his death date, Warfel cites references which indicate

that Brown died on February 21 and was buried February 22. Annie Russell Marble, *Heralds of American Literature* (Chicago, 1907) cites evidence for the burial date (315).

14. Warfel, pp. 108-9, 136-37, 147-48, 162-63, 200-1.

15. Berthoff, " 'A Lesson on Concealment,' " pp. 46-47.

16. For the often quoted passage in which Brown discusses the use of such characters in fiction, see the "Advertisement" for *Sky-Walk,* printed in *The Rhapsodist,* ed. by Warfel, p. 136. Cf. Clark, who makes much of this passage in his criticism of some of the novels (164-65, 171, 173, 181, 183).

17. A notable exception is Warfel, who treats the subject in his discussions not only of *Wieland* but also of *Ormond* and *Jane Talbot* (100-2, 130-31, 136, 198-200). For a contrasting view, see Clark, pp. 168-69, 173.

18. Cf. Warfel, who suggests that Brown's association with John Blair Linn, a minister, may be reflected in this novel (200).

19. "The Editors' Address to the Public," p. 5.

20. Additional evidence of Brown's increasing conservatism is provided by the historical "Sketches," a major portion of which, Berthoff conjectures, dates from about this time and later. See "Charles Brockden Brown's Historical 'Sketches,' " pp. 147-54. We cannot, however, apply the material in the "Sketches" to the novels, any more than we can the passage from *The Literary Magazine.*

Selected Bibliography

PRIMARY SOURCES

This bibliography is selective, stressing Brown's major literary work. It includes the first editions of Brown's important books, the collected editions of his novels, and modern editions of individual works. A number of Brown's fragments are referred to in the footnotes. More complete bibliographies, including Brown's political pamphlets, may be found in the biographies by Warfel and Clark and in Jacob Blanck, *Bibliography of American Literature* (New Haven, 1955), I, 302-9.

1. First Editions

Alcuin: A Dialogue. New York: Printed by T. and J. Swords, 1798. Parts I and II only; Parts III and IV were printed in William Dunlap, *The Life of Charles Brockden Brown* (Philadelphia, 1815), I, 71-105, and as "The Paradise of Women" in the English abridgment of Dunlap's biography, *Memoirs of Charles Brockden Brown, the American Novelist* (London, 1822), pp. 247-308.

Wieland; or, The Transformation. An American Tale. New York: Printed by T. and J. Swords, for H. Caritat, 1798.

Ormond; or, The Secret Witness. New York: Printed by G. Forman, for H. Caritat, 1799.

Arthur Mervyn; or, Memoirs of the Year 1793. Philadelphia: Printed and Published by H. Maxwell, 1799.

Edgar Huntly; or, Memoirs of a Sleep-Walker. Philadelphia: Printed by H. Maxwell, 1799.

Arthur Mervyn; or, Memoirs of the Year 1793. Second Part. New York: Printed and Sold by George F. Hopkins, 1800.

Clara Howard; In a Series of Letters. Philadelphia: Asbury Dickins, 1801. Published in England as *Philip Stanley; or, The Enthusiasm of Love.* London: Lane, Newman, 1807. In the American editions of Brown's collected novels it is entitled *Clara Howard; or, The Enthusiasm of Love.*

Jane Talbot: A Novel. Philadelphia: John Conrad; Baltimore: M. and J. Conrad; Washington City: Rapin, Conrad, 1801.

Carwin, the Biloquist, and Other American Tales and Pieces. London: Henry Colburn, 1822. Brown's two most important fragments, included in this edition, *Memoirs of Carwin, the Biloquist,* and *Memoirs of Stephen Calvert,* had already been printed in William Dunlap, *The Life of Charles Brockden Brown* (Philadelphia, 1815), II, 200-63, 274-472.

2. Collected Editions

The Novels of Charles Brockden Brown. 7 vols. Boston: S. G. Goodrich, 1827.

The Novels of Charles Brockden Brown. 6 vols. Philadelphia: M. Polock, 1857.

Charles Brockden Brown's Novels. 6 vols. Philadelphia: David McKay, 1887. Reprinted Port Washington, N. Y.: Kennikat Press, 1963.

3. *Modern Editions*

Alcuin: A Dialogue. Introduction by LeRoy Elwood Kimball. New Haven: Carl and Margaret Rollins, 1935.

Arthur Mervyn; or, Memoirs of the Year 1793. Edited with an Introduction by Warner Berthoff. Rinehart Edition. New York: Holt, Rinehart and Winston, 1962.

Edgar Huntly; or, Memoirs of a Sleep-Walker. Edited with an Introduction by David Lee Clark. The Modern Readers' Series. New York: Macmillan, 1928.

Ormond. Edited with an Introduction, Chronology, and Bibliography by Ernest Marchand. American Fiction Series. New York: American, 1937. Reprinted New York: Hafner, 1962.

The Rhapsodist and Other Uncollected Writings. Edited with an Introduction by Harry R. Warfel. New York: Scholars' Facsimiles and Reprints, 1943. Includes "The Rhapsodist," "The Man at Home," "A Series of Original Letters," "Advertisement" for *Sky-Walk,* "Extract" from *Sky-Walk,* and "Walstein's School of History."

Wieland; or, The Transformation, together with Memoirs of Carwin, the Biloquist, a Fragment. Edited with an Introduction by Fred Lewis Pattee. American Authors Series. New York: Harcourt, Brace, 1926. Reprinted New York: Hafner, 1958.

SECONDARY SOURCES

This selective bibliography stresses the critical and evaluative studies in preference to the biographical and historical. It includes, however, the major biographies and those critical works which are likely to be most useful to the general student. Other books and articles are cited in the footnotes.

More complete bibliographies are in David Lee Clark, *Charles Brockden Brown: Pioneer Voice of America* (Durham, N. C., 1952); and Spiller, Thorp, *et al., A Literary History of the United States* (New York, 1948), Vol. III and Supplement. Current items may be found in the annual bibliography in *PMLA* and in each issue of *American Literature.*

1. *Biographies*

CLARK, DAVID LEE. *Charles Brockden Brown: Pioneer Voice of America.* Durham, N. C.: Duke University Press, 1952. Reprints material not readily available elsewhere, but devotes relatively little space to criticism of the novels, the treatment of which is sometimes inaccurate and strongly colored by Clark's view of Brown as a proponent of radical ideas.

DUNLAP, WILLIAM. *The Life of Charles Brockden Brown: together with*

Selections from the Rarest of His Printed Works, from His Original Letters, and from His Manuscripts Before Unpublished. Philadelphia: James P. Parke, 1815. Actually begun by Paul Allen and completed by Dunlap. Though inaccurate and disorganized, it is the basis for all subsequent studies of Brown and is particularly valuable for the reprinting of some of Brown's letters and fragments. It was abridged as *Memoirs of Charles Brockden Brown, the American Novelist.* London: Henry Colburn, 1822.

PRESCOTT, WILLIAM HICKLING. "Memoir of Charles Brockden Brown, the American Novelist," *Biographical and Critical Miscellanies.* Philadelphia: J. B. Lippincott, 1865. A brief account of Brown's life and work, appreciative both of his historical importance and of his merits as a writer (first published in 1834). Appears also in Volume III of the collected edition of Brown's novels published in 1887 and reprinted in 1963.

WARFEL, HARRY R. *Charles Brockden Brown: American Gothic Novelist.* Gainesville, Fla.: University of Florida Press, 1949. The most reliable, useful, and readable of the biographies, clearly organized and presented; contains judicious criticism of the novels.

————. *Footnotes to Charles Brockden Brown: American Gothic Novelist (1949).* Gainesville, Fla., 1953. Title page and twelve "dittoed" sheets which present the sources of information and correct a number of statements made in the book.

2. Criticism

BERNARD, KENNETH. "Charles Brockden Brown and the Sublime," *The Personalist,* XLV (1964), 235-49. Points out that although Brown does not describe the American scene realistically but relies rather on eighteenth-century conventions of the sublime and the picturesque, he does make functional use of his descriptions in *Edgar Huntly.*

BERTHOFF, W. B. "Adventures of the Young Man: An Approach to Charles Brockden Brown," *American Quarterly,* IX (1957), 421-34. Considers *Edgar Huntly, Stephen Calvert,* and *Arthur Mervyn* as stories of initiation, but treats only *Arthur Mervyn* and, to a lesser extent, *Stephen Calvert* in detail.

————. "'A Lesson on Concealment': Brockden Brown's Method in Fiction," *Philological Quarterly,* XXXVII (1958), 45-57. Describes Brown's fictional method as a means for testing ideas in terms of human motives and actions, and illustrates its contention through an analysis of one of Brown's short stories.

————. "Charles Brockden Brown's Historical 'Sketches': A Consideration," *American Literature,* XXVIII (1956), 147-54. Argues that a major portion of the "Sketches" was probably written much later than has generally been supposed, and interprets them as basically conservative documents.

BLAKE, WARREN BARTON. "Brockden Brown and the Novel," *Sewanee Review,* XVIII (1910), 431-43. Treats Brown as a transitional figure "who stood on the boundary line between the old-fashioned and the modern novel."

CHANNING, E. T. "Charles Brockden Brown," *North American Review*, IX (1819), 58-77. An early, but still useful, discussion of the strengths and weaknesses of Brown's fiction (actually, a review of Dunlap's biography).

CHASE, RICHARD. *The American Novel and Its Tradition*. New York: Doubleday, 1957. Good discussions of *Wieland* and *Edgar Huntly*, but more important for its treatment of Brown as the forerunner, in his use of melodrama, of a major strain in the American novel.

COWIE, ALEXANDER. *The Rise of the American Novel*. New York: American, 1951. A balanced account of Brown's life and works with comment on his social views, literary theory, and reputation.

DAVIS, DAVID BRION. *Homicide in American Fiction, 1798-1860: A Study in Social Values*. Ithaca, N. Y.: Cornell University Press, 1957. Discusses *Wieland* and *Edgar Huntly* at some length, but leans rather heavily on modern psychological theory in interpreting them.

FIEDLER, LESLIE A. *Love and Death in the American Novel*. New York: Criterion Books, 1960. Discusses Brown's novels–most particularly *Edgar Huntly*–in terms of the Sentimental and Gothic traditions, but not always accurate in detail; strongly colored, of course, by Fiedler's critical assumptions.

LEWIS, R. W. B. *The American Adam: Innocence, Tragedy, and Tradition in the Nineteenth Century*. Chicago: University of Chicago Press, 1955. Discusses *Arthur Mervyn* as an initiation story which introduces the Adam figure into American literature in the person of the hero.

LOSHE, LILLIE DEMING. *The Early American Novel*. New York: Columbia University Press, 1907. Stresses the influence of Godwin and the Illuminati, and Brown's use of native materials.

MANLY, WILLIAM M. "The Importance of Point of View in Brockden Brown's *Wieland*," *American Literature*, XXXV (1963), 311-21. An interpretation of the novel which focuses upon Clara as the central character who is brought to the point of madness by the conflict between the rational and non-rational elements in her make-up.

MARCHAND, ERNEST. "The Literary Opinions of Charles Brockden Brown," *Studies in Philology*, XXXI (1934), 541-66. Discusses Brown's literary opinions as they can be culled from his books and from articles attributed to him with reasonable certainty; concludes that Brown's criticism is of slight importance.

NEAL, JOHN. *American Writers: A Series of Papers Contributed to Blackwood's Magazine (1824-1825)*. Ed. by Fred Lewis Pattee. Durham, N. C.: Duke University Press, 1937. Early appreciation of Brown's genius and, despite his faults, of his power as a writer.

SNELL, GEORGE. *The Shapers of American Fiction, 1798-1947*. New York: E. P. Dutton, 1947. Places Brown at the head of what he calls the apocalyptic strain of American fiction and includes some brief discussions of the novels, most particularly *Arthur Mervyn*.

TILTON, ELEANOR M. "'The Sorrows' of Charles Brockden Brown," *PMLA*, LXIX (1954), 1304-8. Argues that the letters to Henrietta G., usually taken as biographical data, are really an attempt at an epistolary novel in the *Werther* vein.

Selected Bibliography

VILAS, MARTIN S. *Charles Brockden Brown: A Study of Early American Fiction.* Burlington, Vt.: Free Press Association, 1904. The first attempt at a systematic study of Brown's fiction and its influence; treatment of the novels in rather sketchy.

WARFEL, HARRY R. "Charles Brockden Brown's German Sources," *Modern Language Quarterly,* I (1940), 357-65. Important in locating a possible source for *Wieland* from which Brown may have derived his use of sensationalist psychology.

ZIFF, LARZER. "A Reading of *Wieland,*" *PMLA,* LXXVII (1962), 51-57. Maintains that in turning away from some of the presuppositions of his age, Brown, in *Wieland,* foreshadows both "the theme and the manner" of subsequent American fiction.

Index

Characters in the novels are not included here unless referred to in discussions other than those of the specific novels in which they appear.